FINGERPRINTS

14 easy contemporary pieces for cello and piano

14 leichte zeitgenössische Stücke für Cello und Klavier

14 morceaux faciles et contemporains pour violoncelle et piano

Cello part

CONTENTS

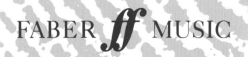

FABER *ff* MUSIC

FOREWORD

WELCOME TO *FINGERPRINTS* for cello, a sparkling collection of pieces commissioned especially for cellists from some very imaginative, alive and kicking 21st-century composers.

Learning the notes is only the beginning and something very special happens at the next stage – the performance. It doesn't matter where – the living room, the school assembly, the exam room, a music festival or the concert hall. Give these pieces an audience and something magical happens; the piece unfolds and changes with each performance.

Do try the accompanied pieces out with piano, even in the early stages of learning, to give yourself a full idea of the atmosphere and texture the piece is meant to convey. This will really help you to play with more feeling and expression. (The piano parts are specially designed so that you won't need the services of a concert pianist!)

Wishing you an exciting journey of discovery in the pages ahead.

All of the composers were asked to provide their full name, date of birth and two of their 'favourite things' – the answers are shown on the respective music pages. Here are my answers:

Full name **William Bruce**   *Date and place of birth* **23.10.57; Sunderland**
Favourite drink **raspberry and blueberry smoothie**   *Favourite sound* **the African bush at dusk**

© 2006 by Faber Music Ltd
First published in 2006 by Faber Music Ltd
Bloomsbury House
74–77 Great Russell Street
London WC1B 3DA
Cover design by Nick Flower
Music processed by Jackie Leigh
Printed in England by Caligraving Ltd
All rights reserved

ISBN10: 0-571-52297-1
EAN13: 978-0-571-52297-2

To buy Faber Music publications or to find out about the full range of titles available please contact your local music retailer or Faber Music sales enquiries:

Faber Music Limited, Burnt Mill, Elizabeth Way, Harlow, CM20 2HX England
Tel: +44 (0)1279 82 89 82   Fax: +44 (0)1279 82 89 83
sales@fabermusic.com   fabermusicstore.com

Full name **Christian David Alexander**   *Date and place of birth* 15.1.64; Liverpool
Favourite instrument **human voice**   *Favourite fast food* **pizza**

Curious minuet

Christian Alexander

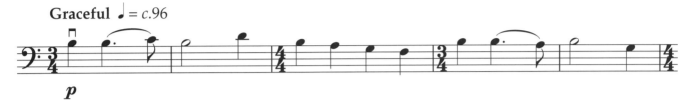

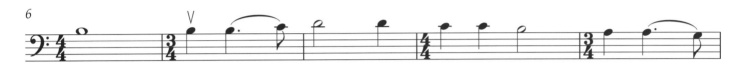

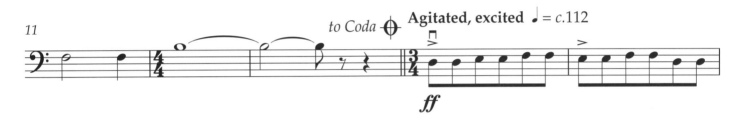

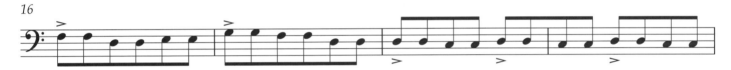

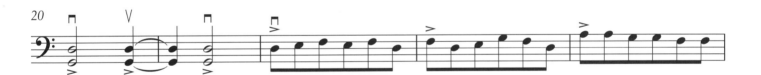

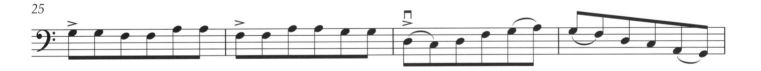

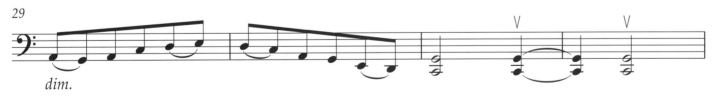

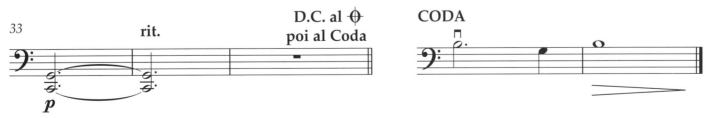

Full name **Ruth Mary Byrchmore**   *Date and place of birth* **19.4.66; Birmingham**
Favourite sweet **chocolate eclairs**   *Favourite instrument* **piano**

NYPD TV (cello solo)

Ruth Byrchmore

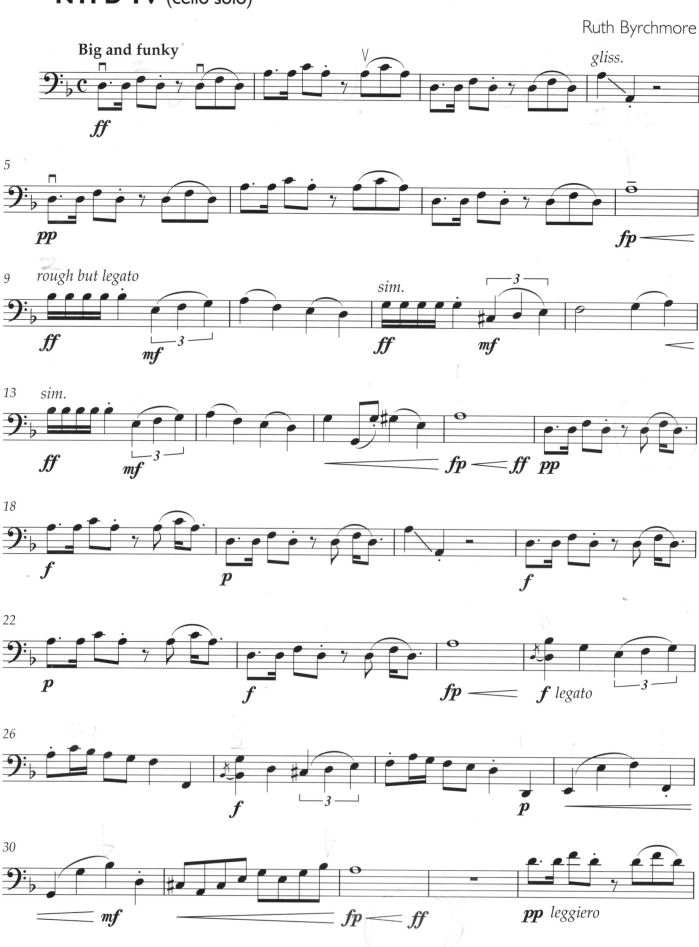

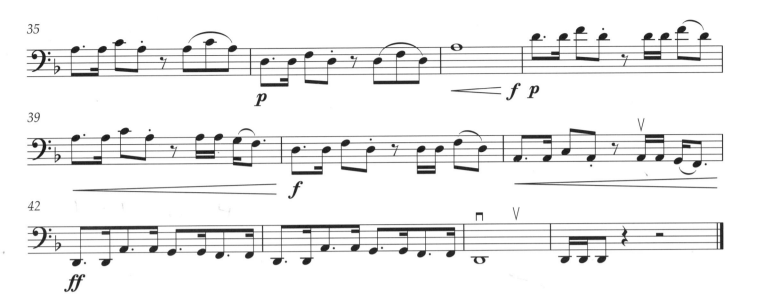

Full name Charles Hay Dickie   *Date and place of birth* **22.9.49; London**
Favourite animal **jaguar**   *Favourite book* **Attention All Shipping** by Charlie Connelly

Ghost note

Charles Dickie

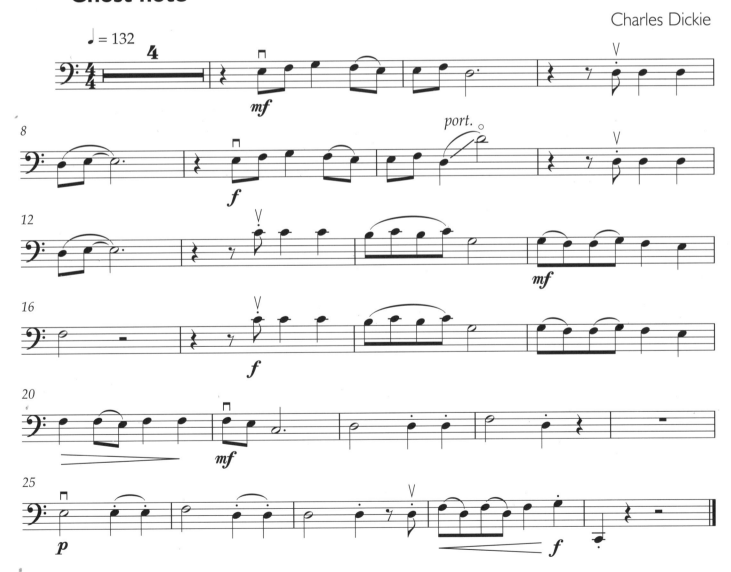

Full name **Charles Hay Dickie**   *Date and place of birth* **22.9.49; London**
Favourite animal **jaguar**   *Favourite book* **Attention All Shipping** by Charlie Connelly

Texting (cello solo)

Charles Dickie

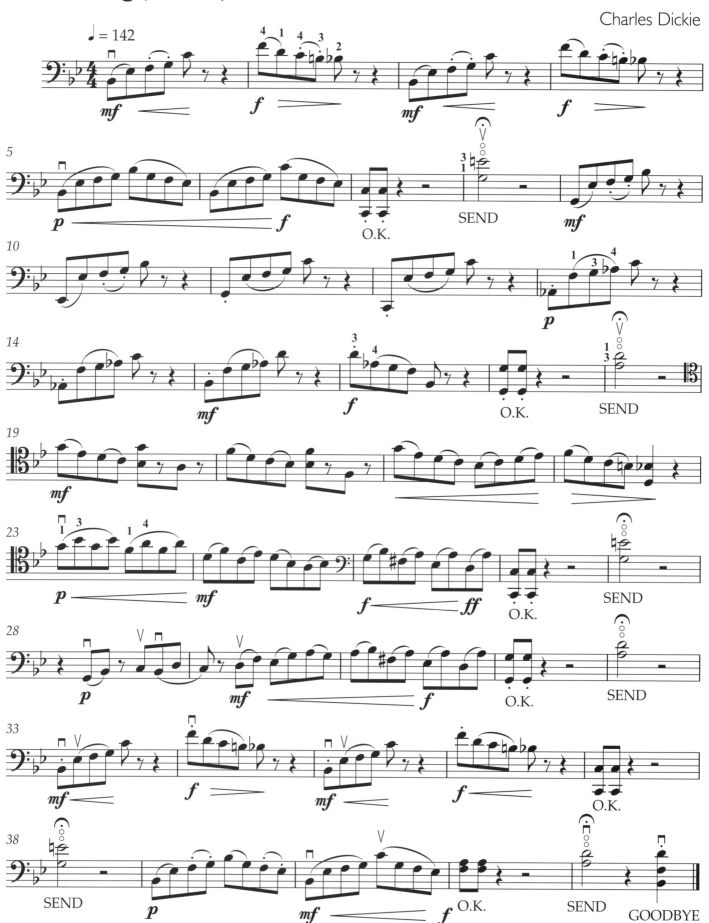

Full name **Howard (L.) Goodall**   *Date and place of birth* **26.5.58; South Bromley**

Favourite football team **Newcastle United (black and white)**   *Favourite sweet* **Milky Way**

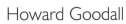

Secret places

Howard Goodall

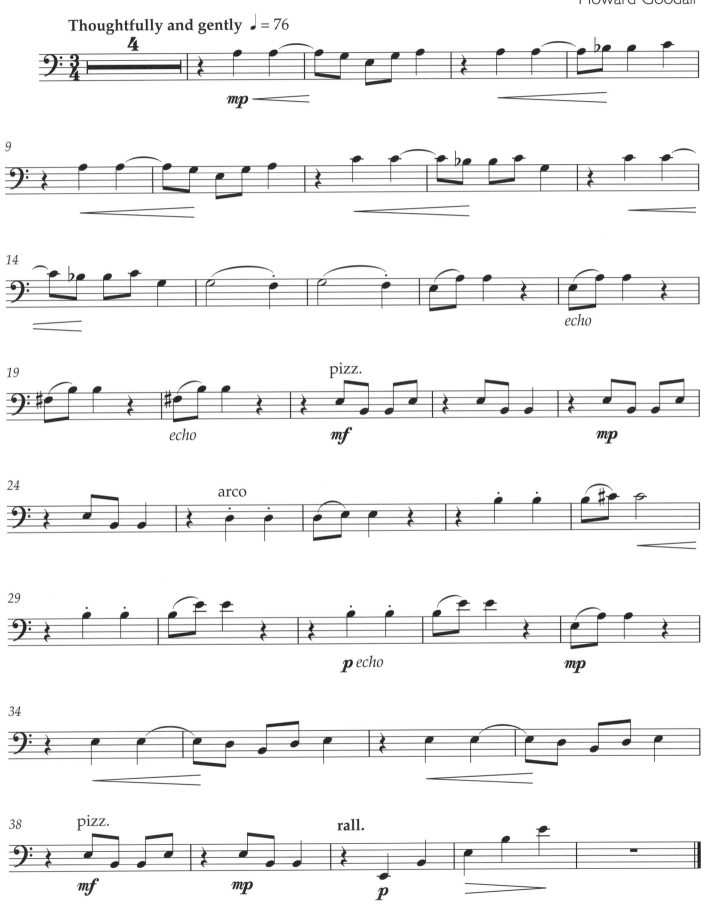

Full name **Paul Brian Hart**   *Date and place of birth* **16.3.54; London**
Favourite sound **the violin, or my dog snoring**   *Favourite hobby* **driving my car, for pleasure**

Bonjour tristesse

Paul Hart

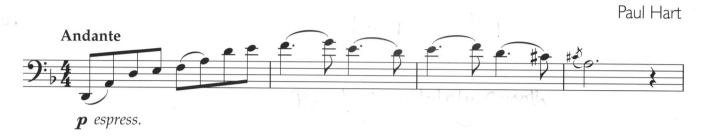

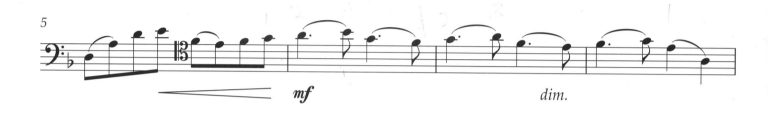

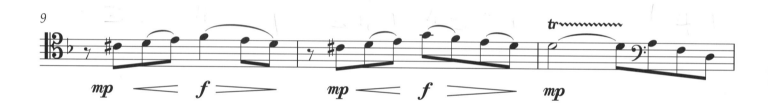

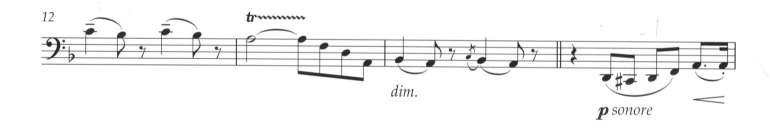

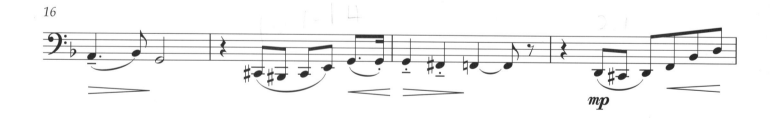

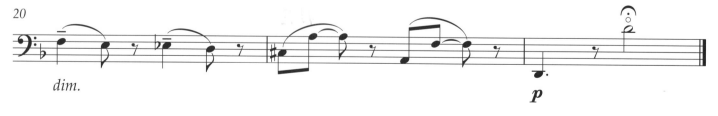

Full name **Matthew John Hindson**   *Date and place of birth* **12.9.68; Port Kembla, New South Wales, Australia**
Favourite pudding **chocolate self-saucing pudding**   *Favourite colour* **dark blue**

Zig zag

Matthew Hindson

As fast as possible ♩ = up to 90

Big

Full name **Stephen Andrew Gill Hough**   *Date and place of birth* **22.11.61; Heswall**
Favourite animal **Italian greyhound**   *Favourite book* ***The Professor's House*** by Willa Cather and other novels of hers

to Pauline for Gabriel, cello and Steven, piano

From the sea

Stephen Hough

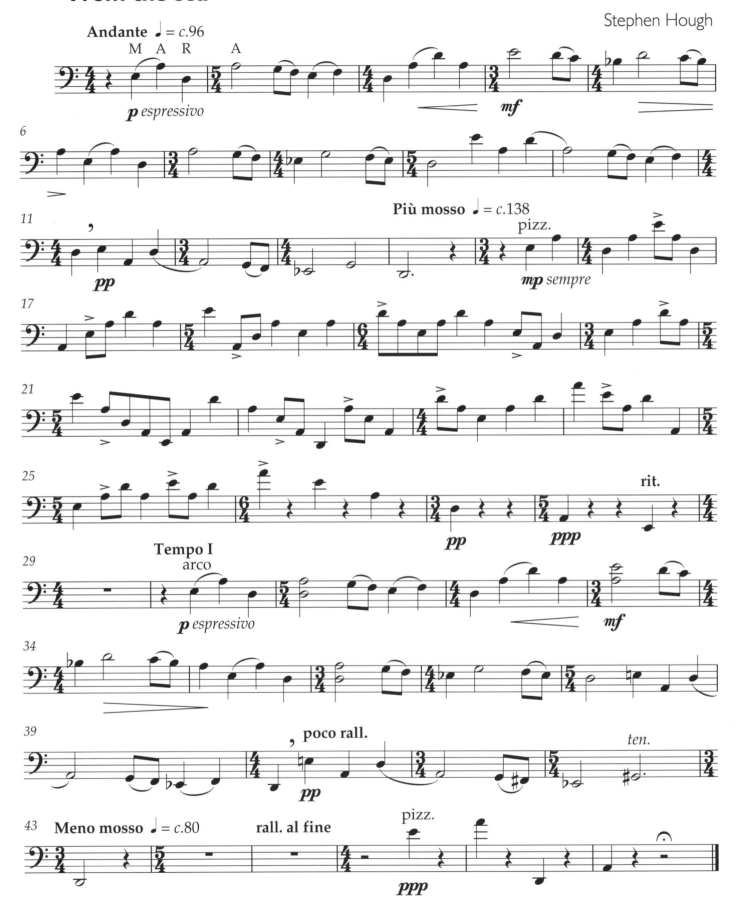

Full name **Nicola Anne Churchill**   *Date and place of birth* **16.5.63; Dunstable**
Favourite piece of music ***Turn out the Stars*** by Bill Evans   *Favourite colour* **green**

The wishing gate

Nikki Iles

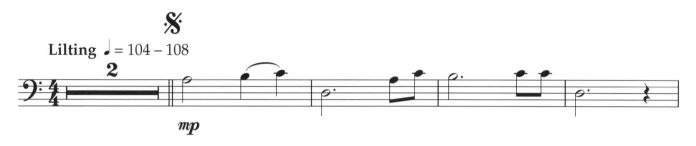

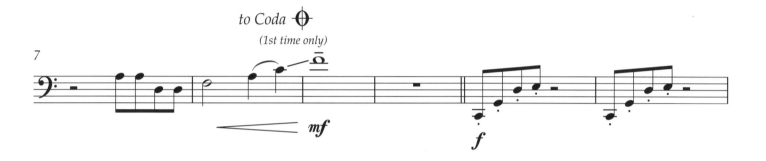

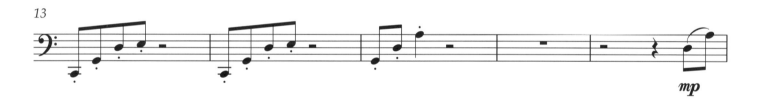

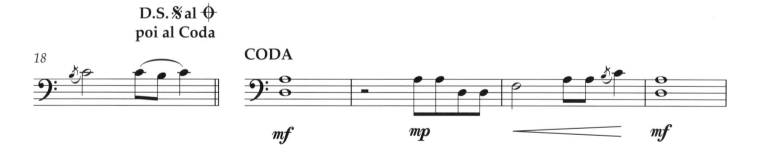

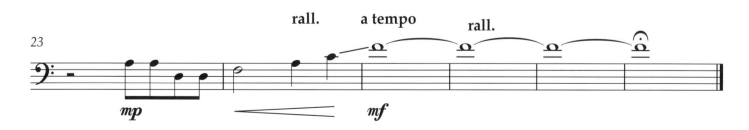

Full name **Thomas Spencer Hewitt Jones**   *Date and place of birth* **24.10.84; Denmark Hill, London**

Favourite day of the week **Wednesday**   *Favourite drink* **raspberry smoothie**

Song of the rose

Thomas Hewitt Jones

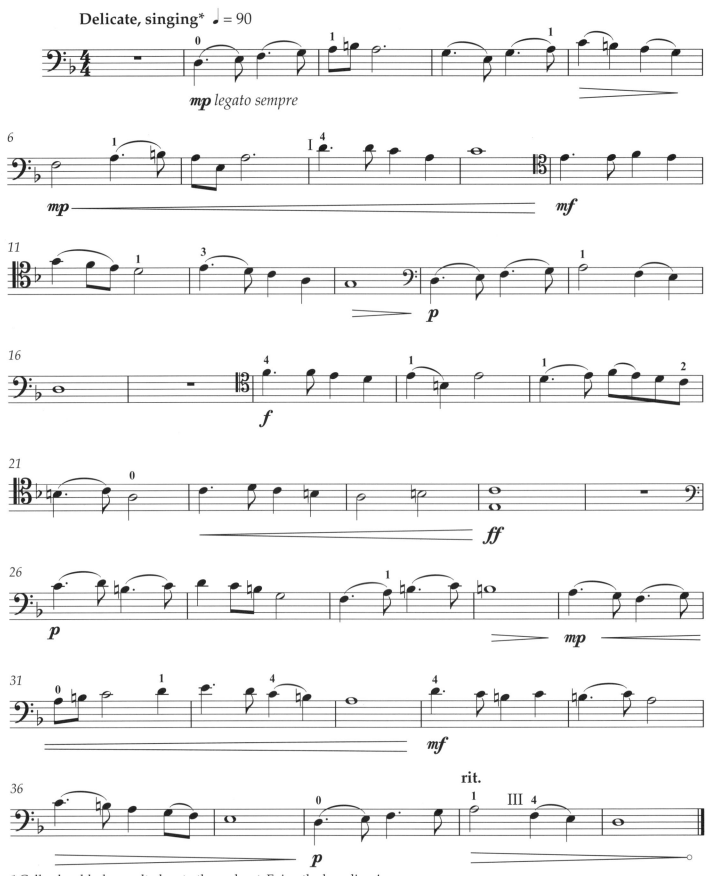

* Cello should play molto legato throughout. Enjoy the long lines!

FINGERPRINTS

14 easy contemporary pieces for cello and piano

14 leichte zeitgenössische Stücke für Cello und Klavier
14 morceaux faciles et contemporains pour violoncelle et piano

Piano accompaniment

CONTENTS

© 2006 by Faber Music Ltd
First published in 2006 by Faber Music Ltd
Bloomsbury House
74–77 Great Russell Street
London WC1B 3DA
Cover design by Nick Flower
Music processed by Jackie Leigh
Printed in England by Caligraving Ltd

ISBN10: 0-571-52297-1
EAN13: 978-0-571-52297-2

To buy Faber Music publications or to find out about the full range of titles available
please contact your local music retailer or Faber Music sales enquiries:

Faber Music Limited, Burnt Mill, Elizabeth Way, Harlow, CM20 2HX England
Tel: +44 (0)1279 82 89 82   Fax: +44 (0)1279 82 89 83
sales@fabermusic.com   fabermusicstore.com

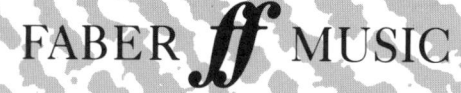

FABER ff MUSIC

Curious minuet

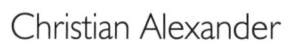

Christian Alexander

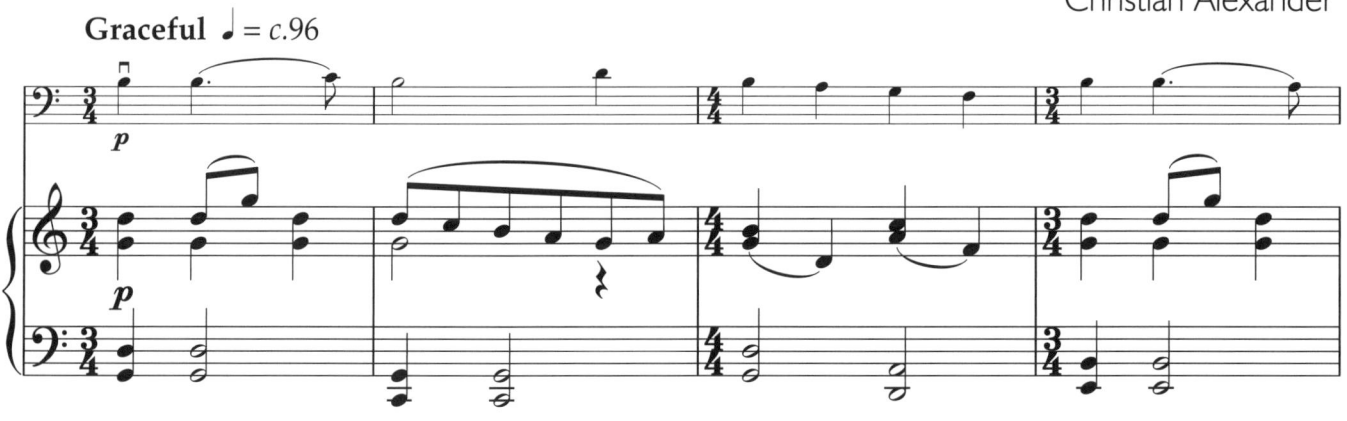

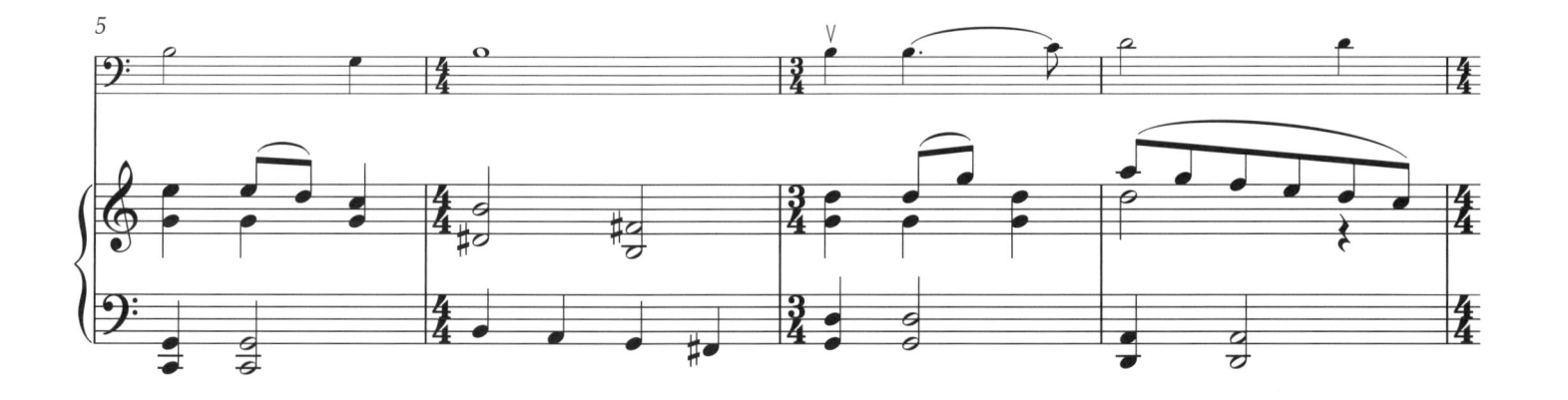

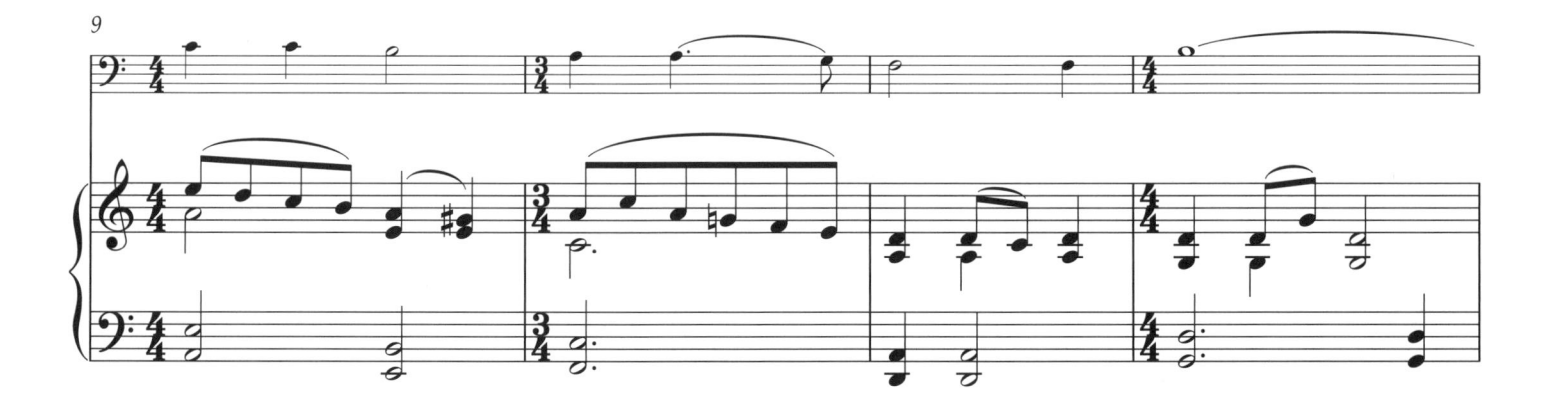

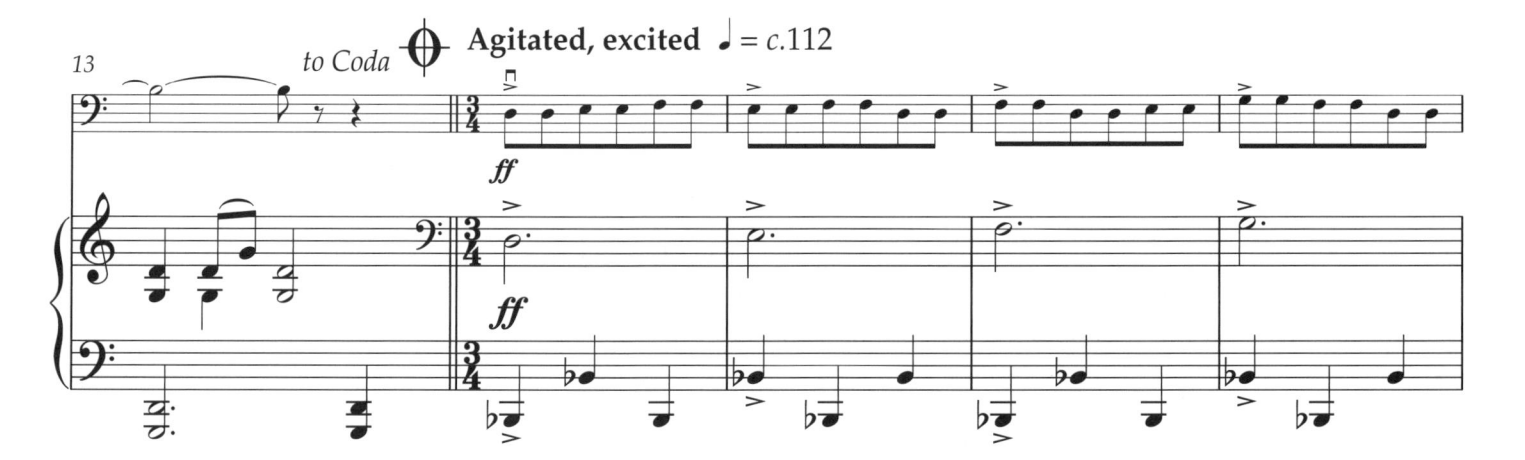

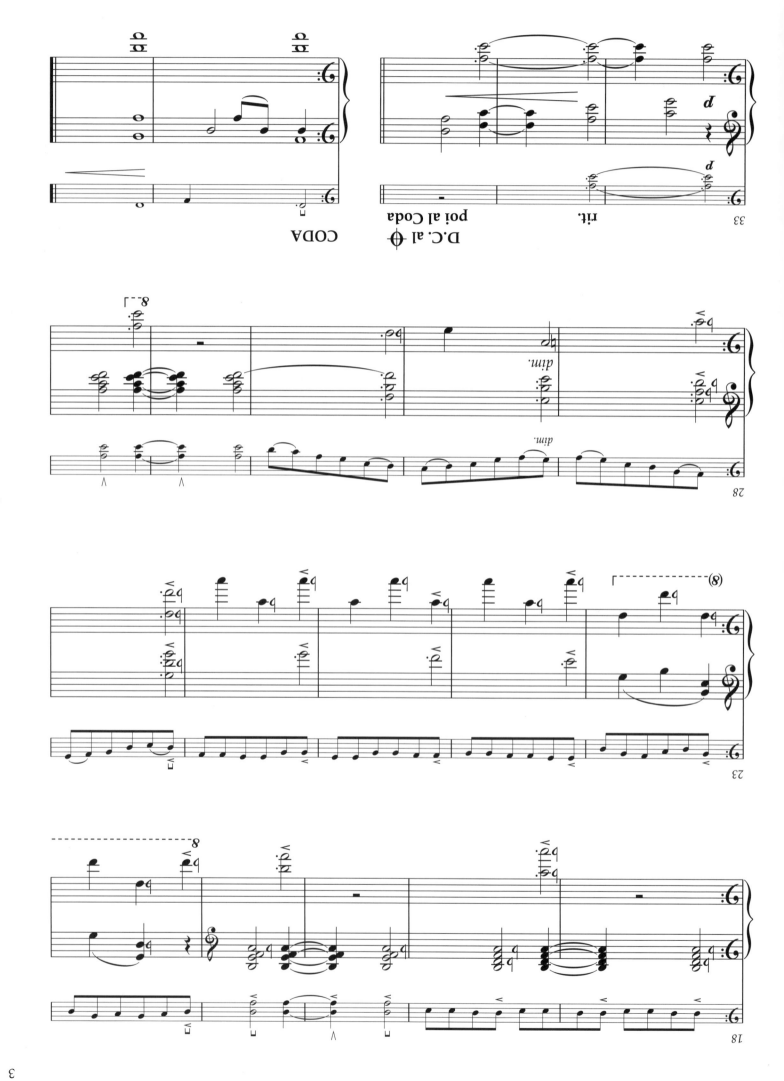

Full name **Charles Hay Dickie** *Date and place of birth* **22.9.49; London**
Favourite animal **jaguar** *Favourite book* ***Attention All Shipping*** by Charlie Connelly

Ghost note

Charles Dickie

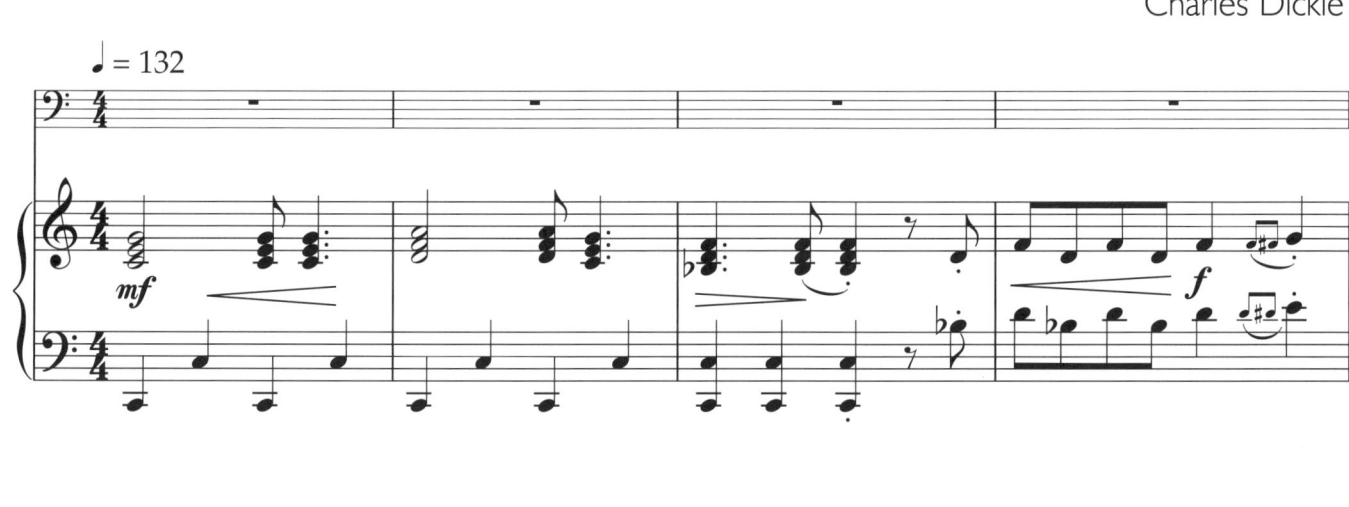

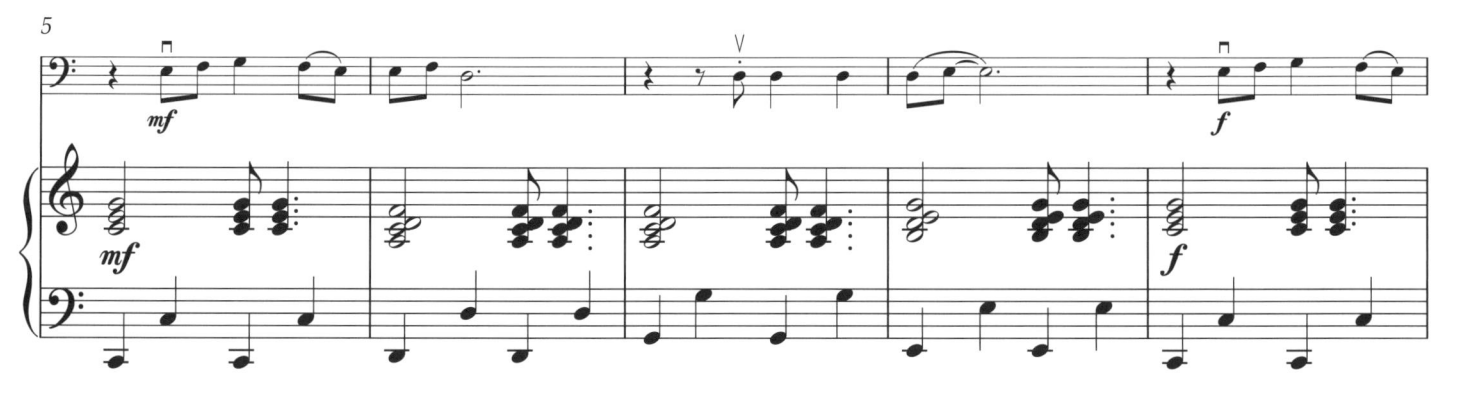

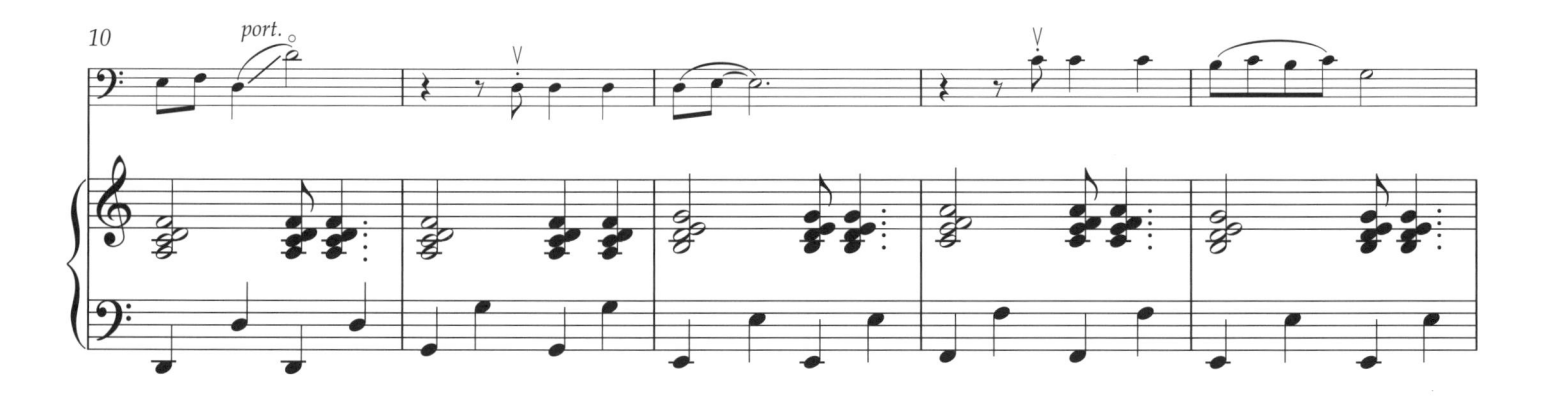

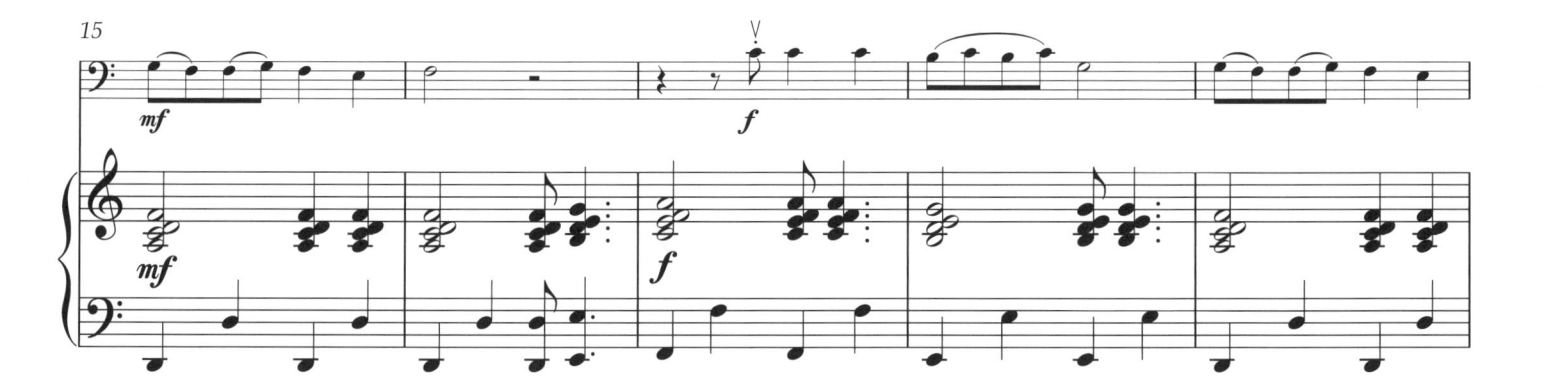

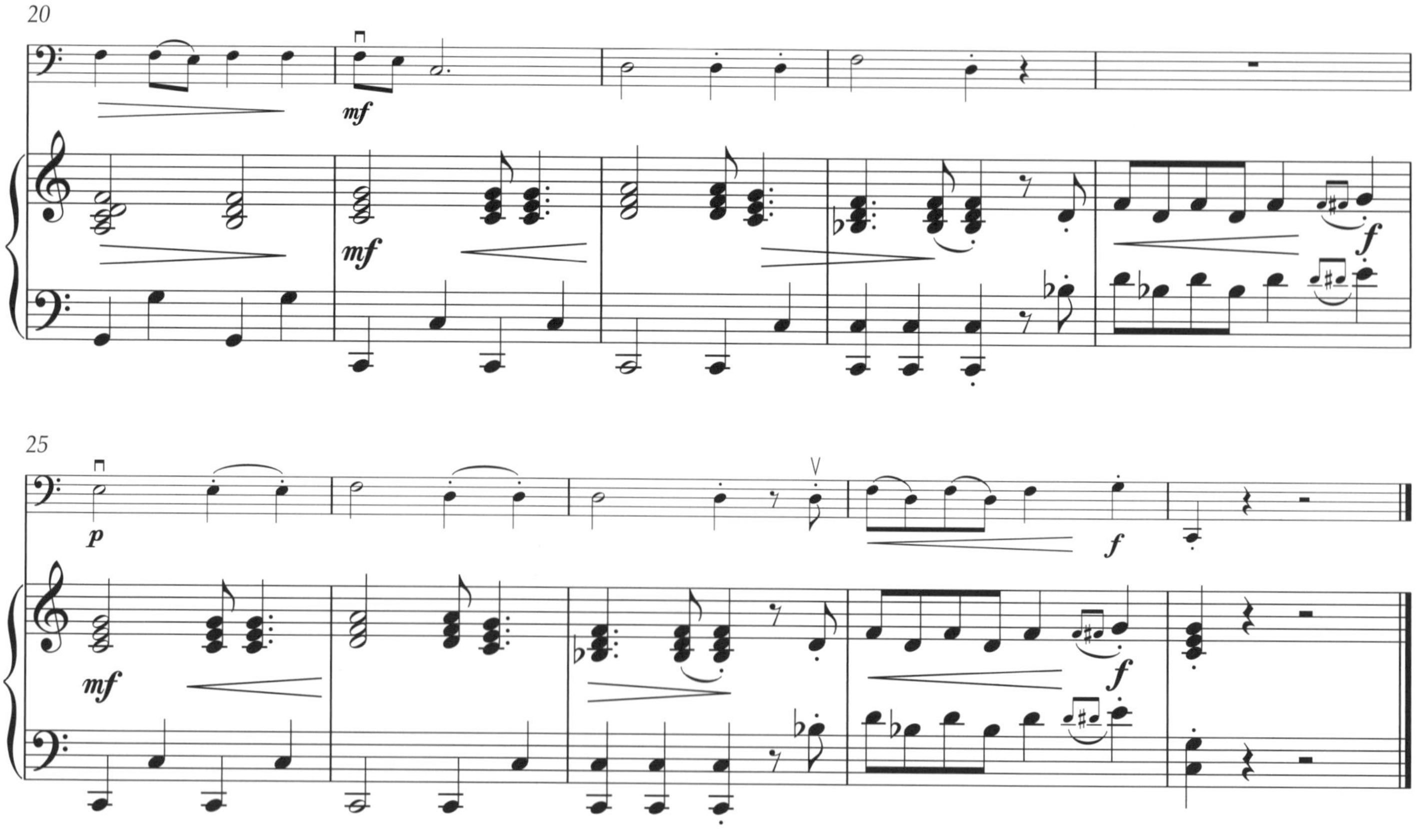

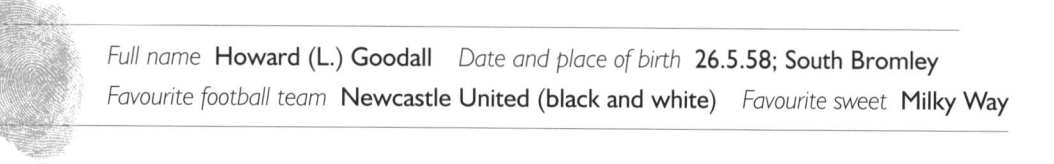

Full name **Howard (L.) Goodall** Date and place of birth **26.5.58; South Bromley**
Favourite football team **Newcastle United (black and white)** Favourite sweet **Milky Way**

Secret places

Howard Goodall

Thoughtfully and gently ♩ = 76

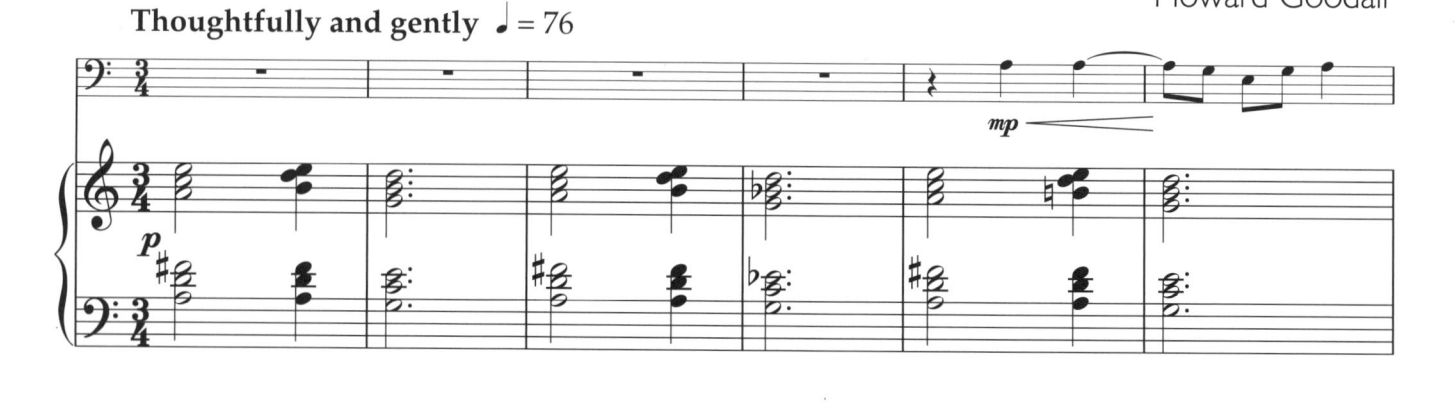

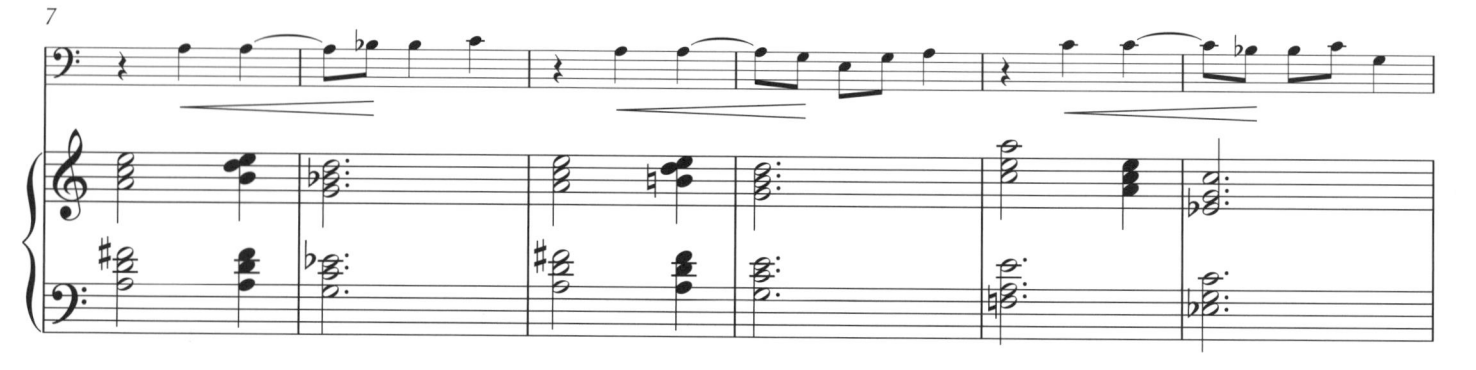

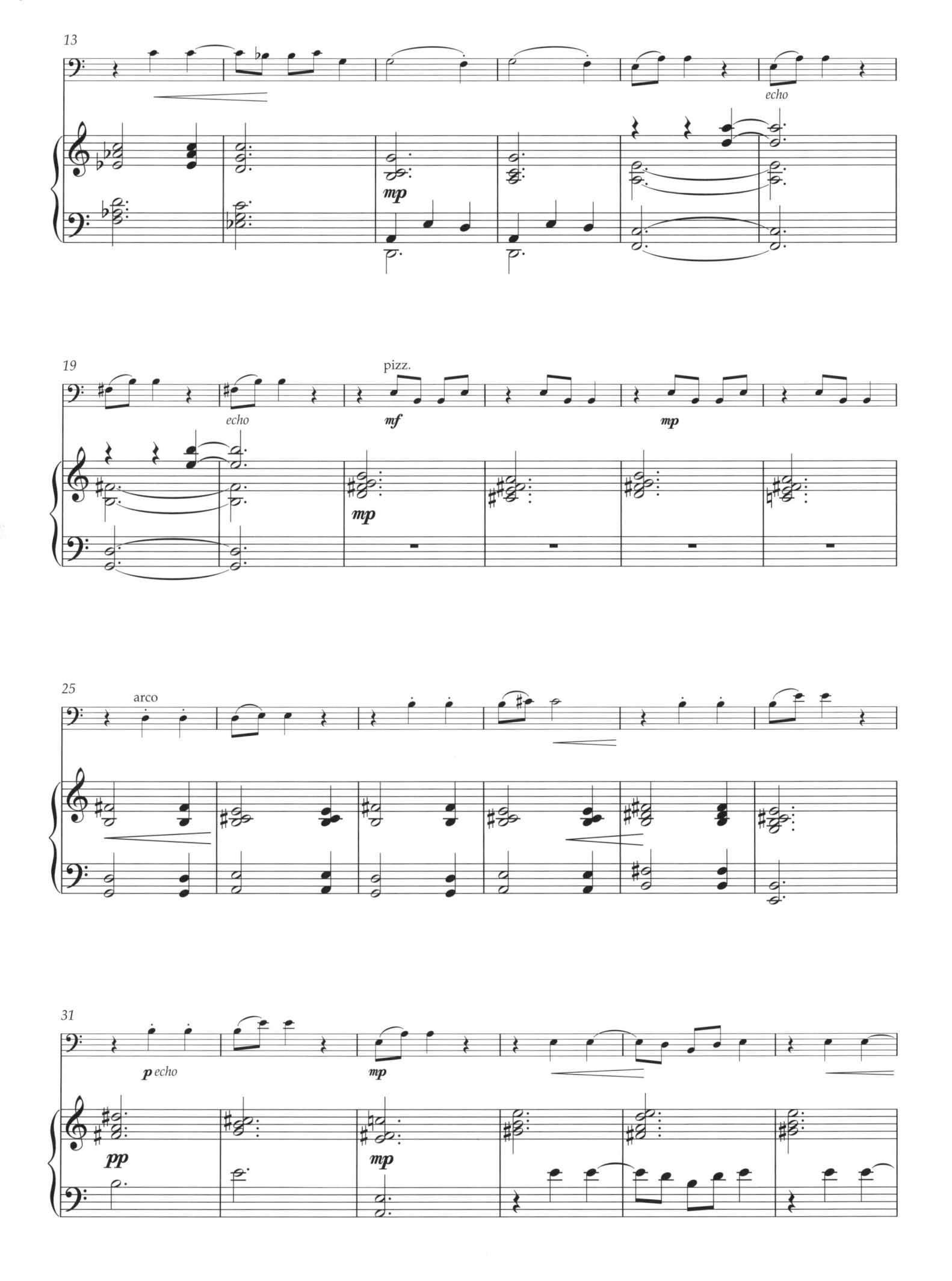

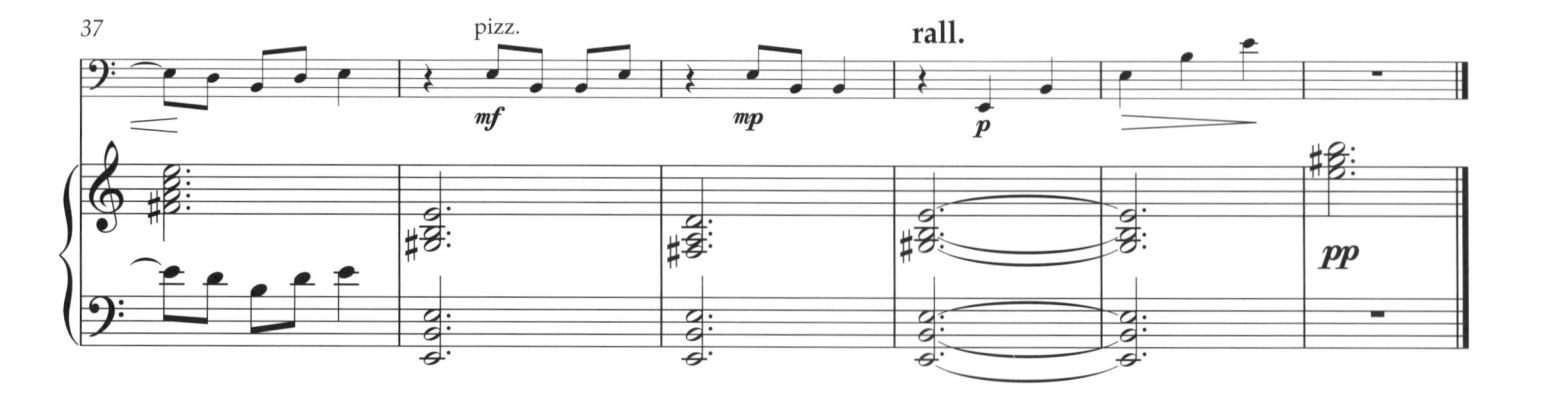

Full name **Paul Brian Hart**   *Date and place of birth* **16.3.54; London**
Favourite sound **the violin, or my dog snoring**   *Favourite hobby* **driving my car, for pleasure**

Bonjour tristesse

Paul Hart

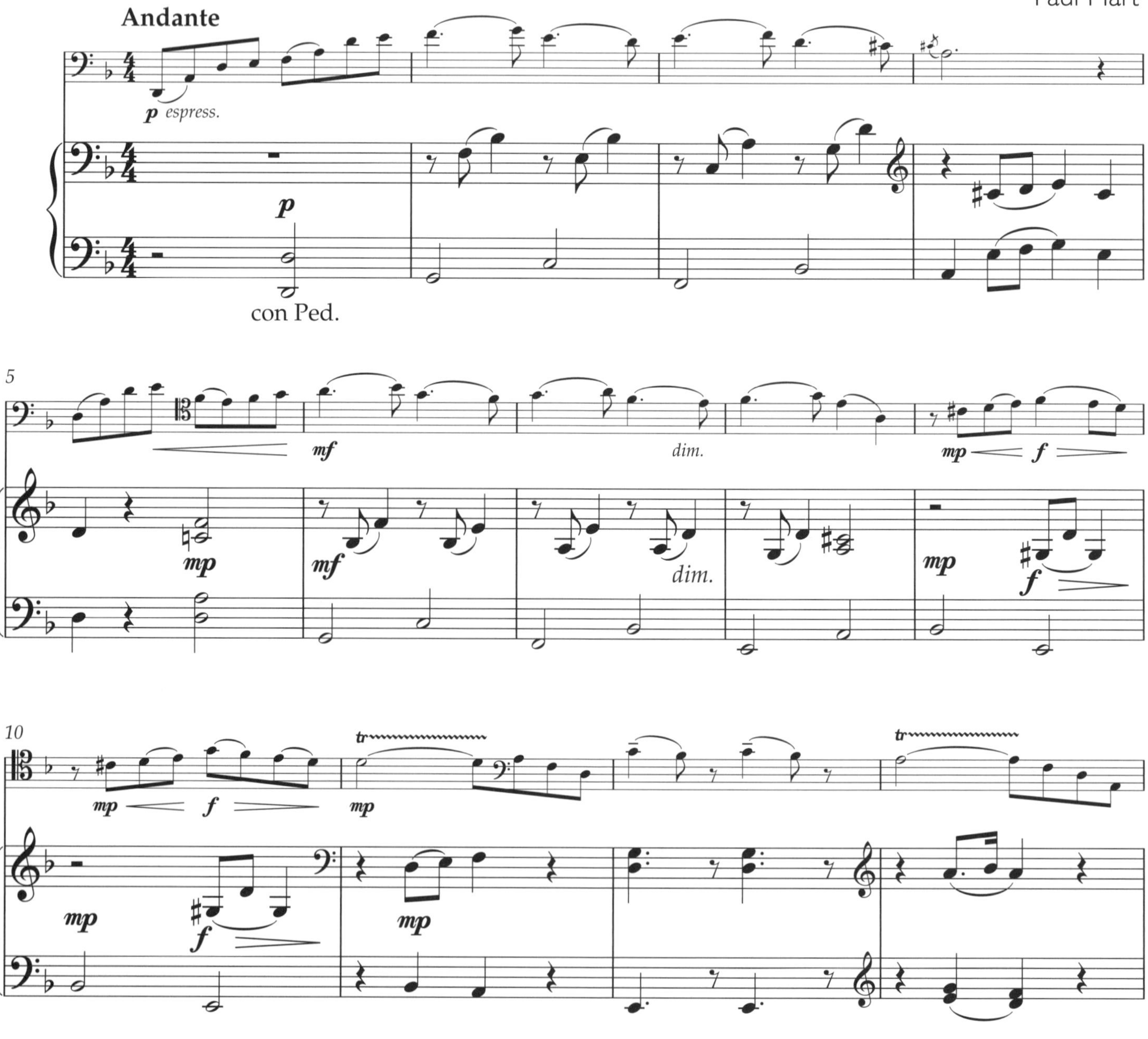

8

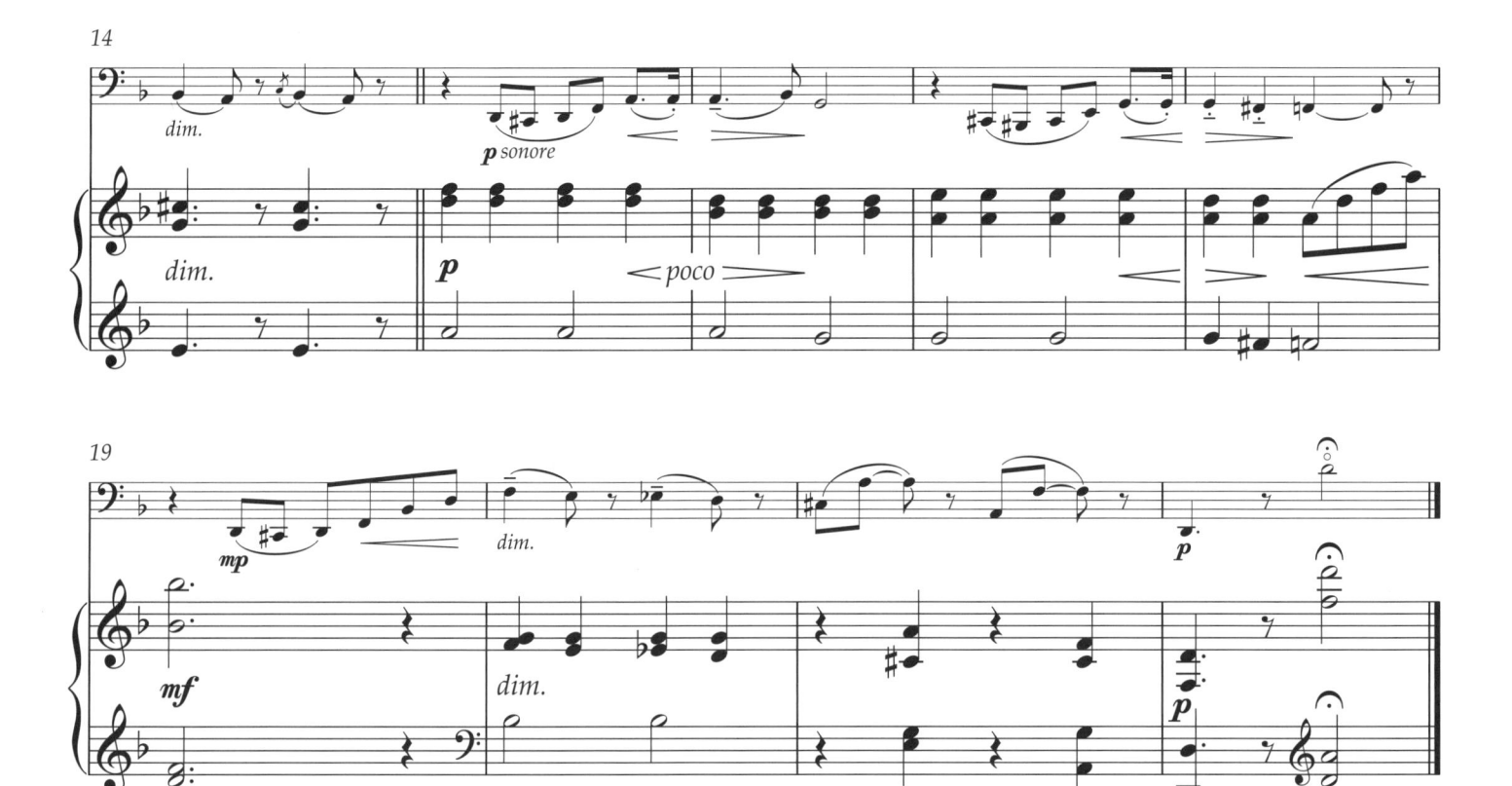

Full name **Matthew John Hindson**   *Date and place of birth* **12.9.68; Port Kembla, New South Wales, Australia**
Favourite pudding **chocolate self-saucing pudding**   *Favourite colour* **dark blue**

Zig zag

Matthew Hindson

As fast as possible ♩ = up to 90

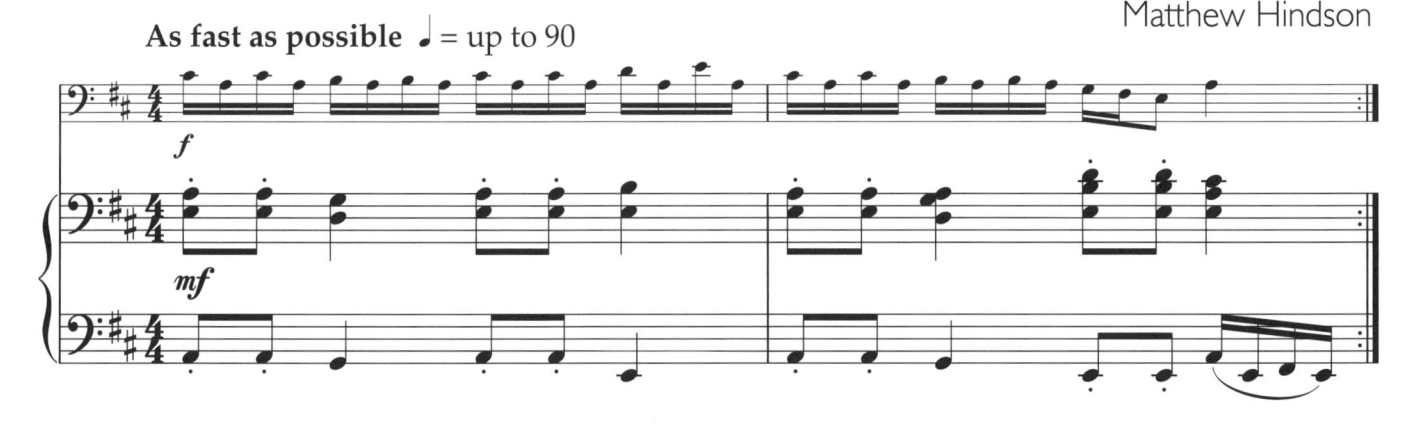

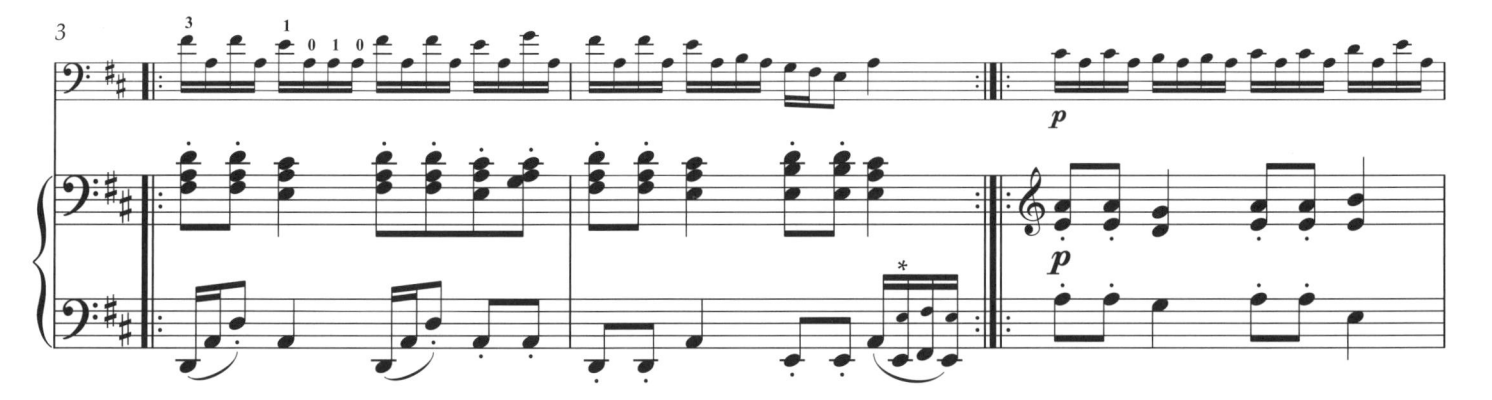

* Play cue size notes on repeat.

© 2006 by Faber Music Ltd.

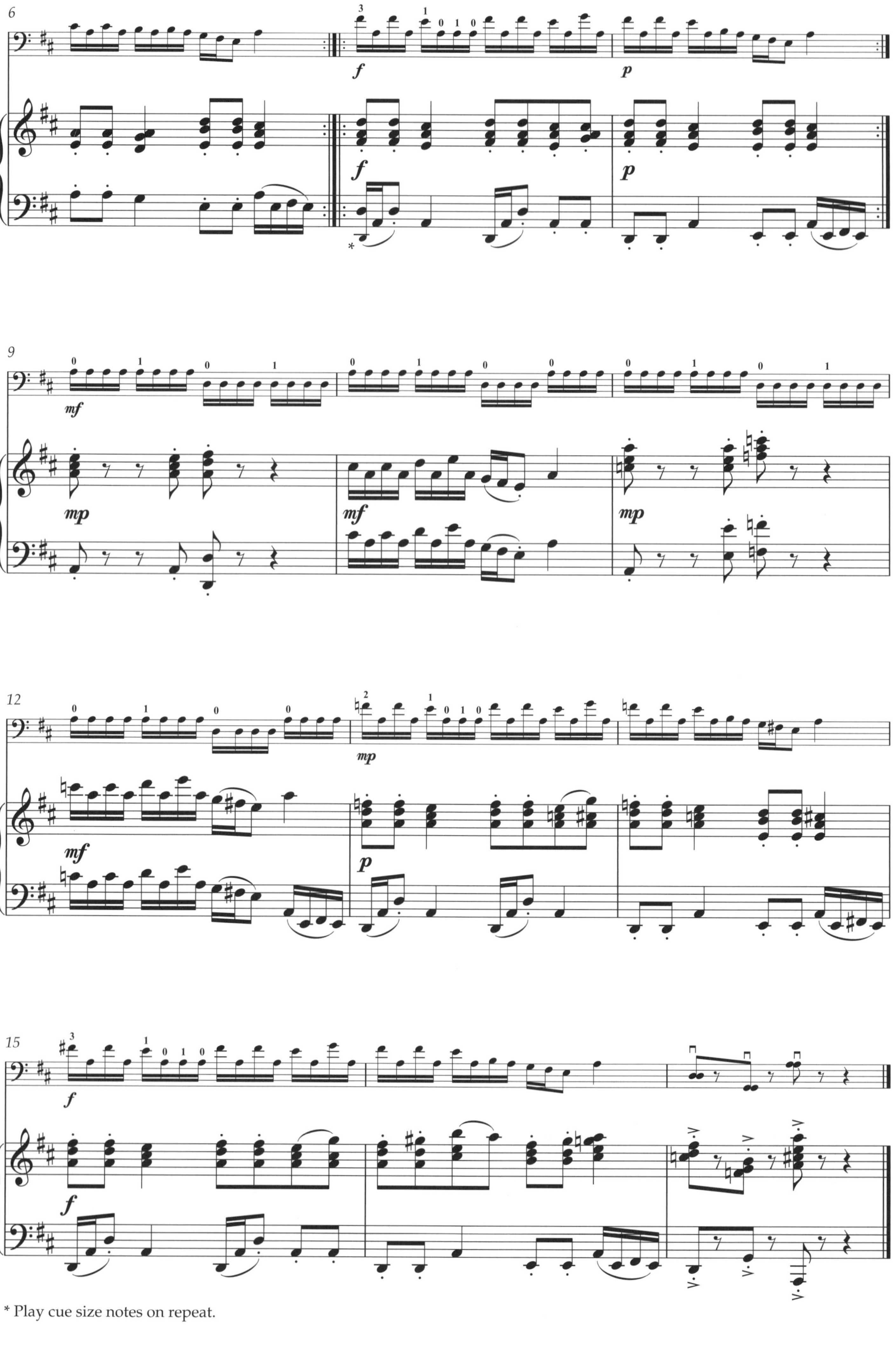

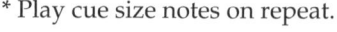

* Play cue size notes on repeat.

Full name **Stephen Andrew Gill Hough**   *Date and place of birth* **22.11.61; Heswall**

Favourite animal **Italian greyhound**   *Favourite book* **The Professor's House** by Willa Cather and other novels of hers

to Pauline for Gabriel, cello and Steven, piano

From the sea

Stephen Hough

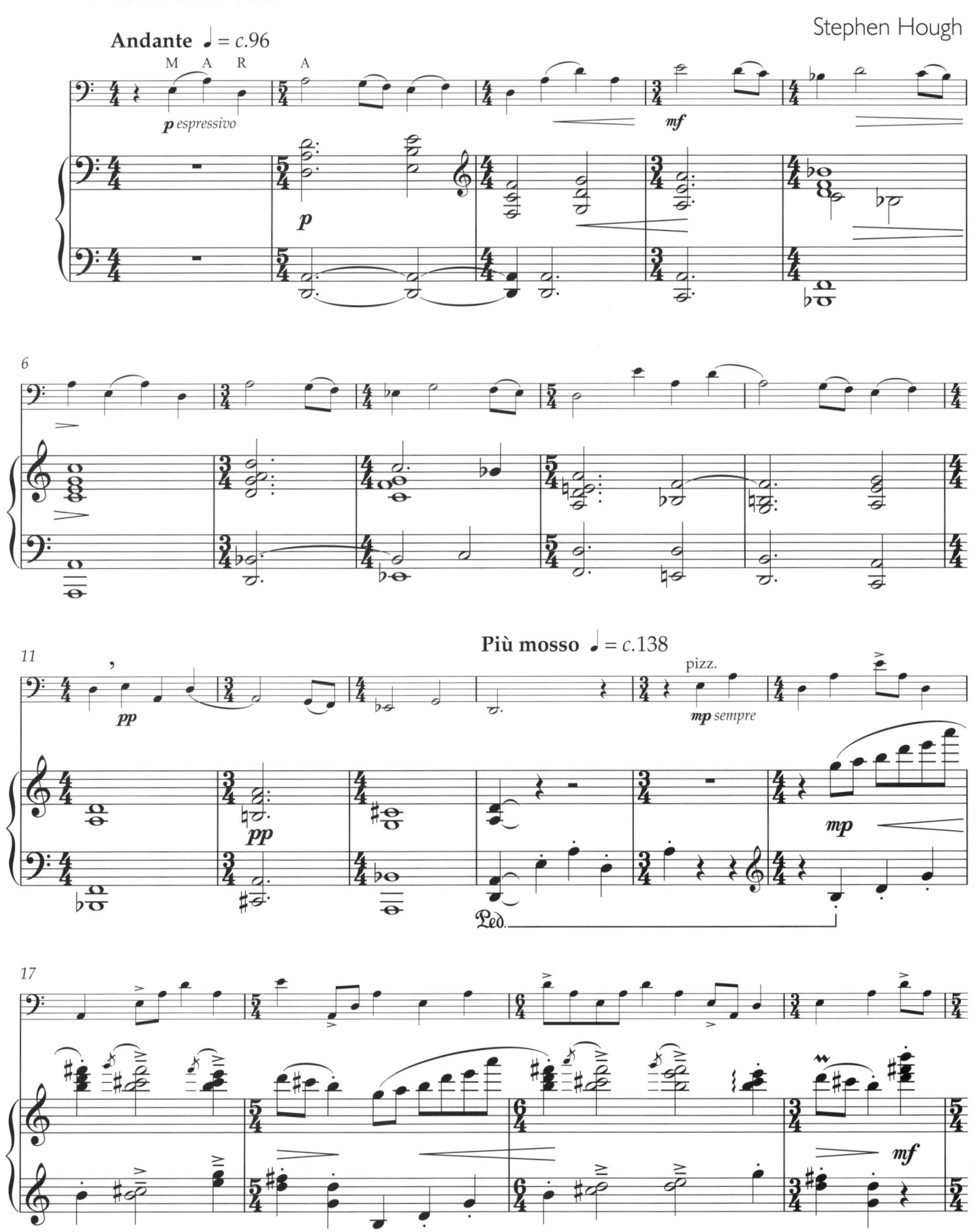

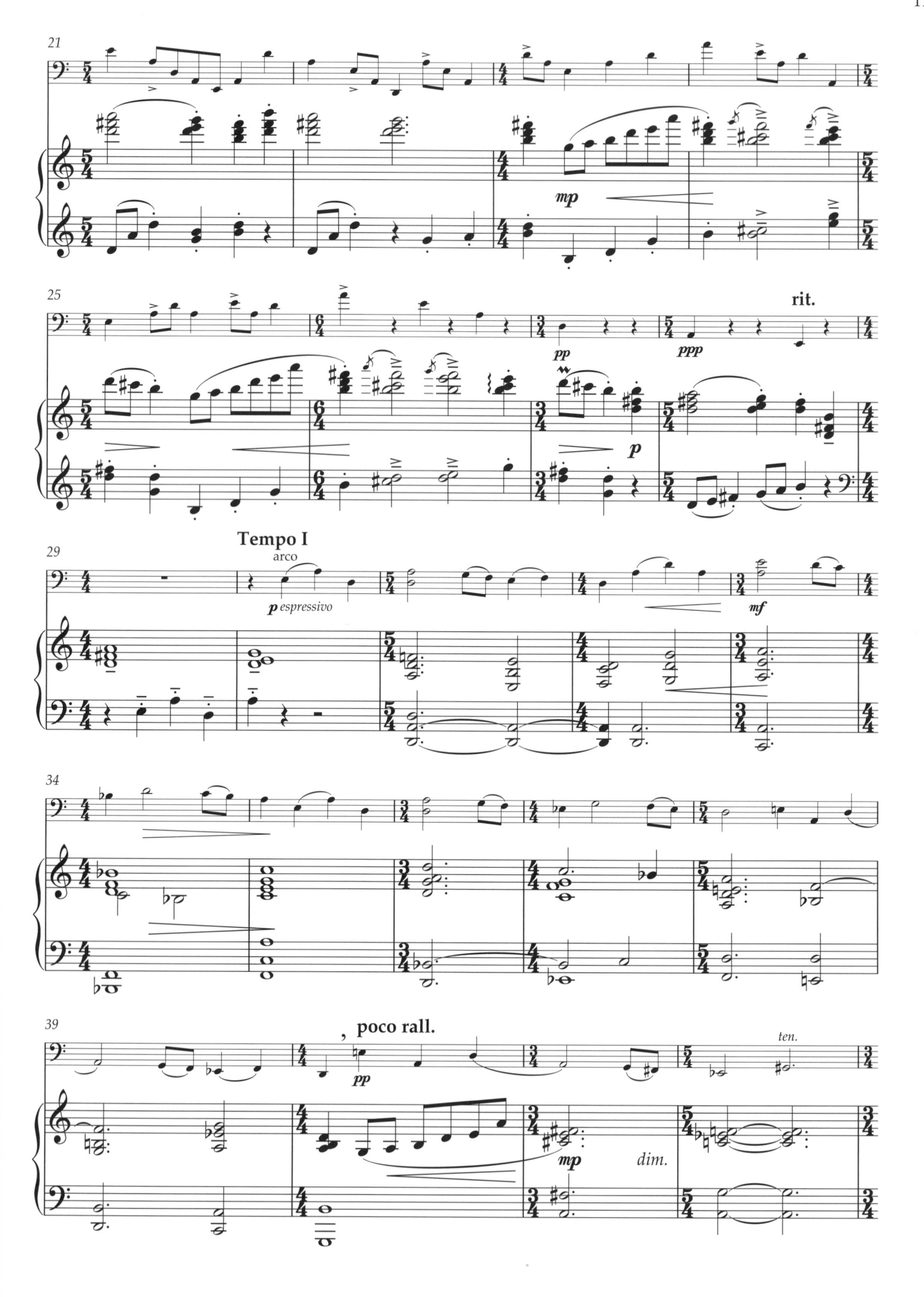

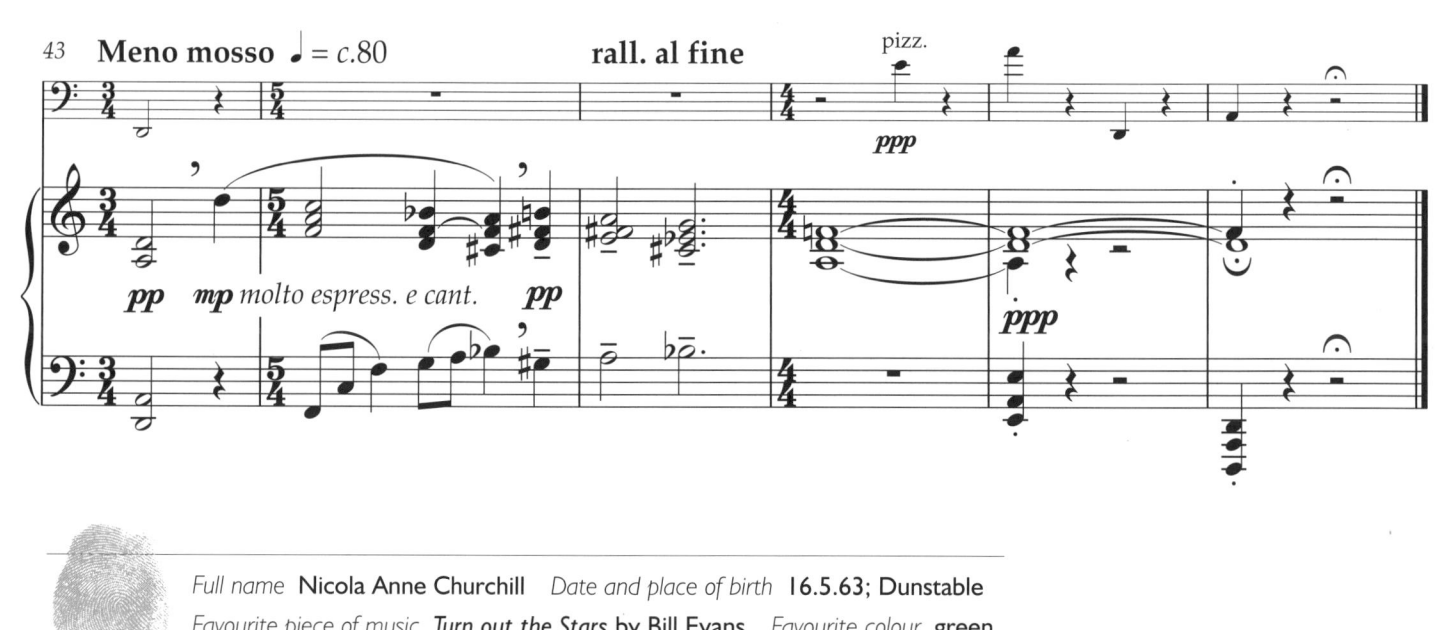

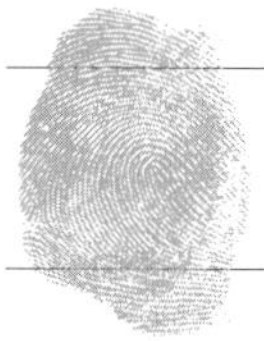

43 **Meno mosso** ♩= *c*.80   rall. al fine

Full name **Nicola Anne Churchill**   Date and place of birth **16.5.63; Dunstable**
Favourite piece of music *Turn out the Stars* by Bill Evans   Favourite colour **green**

The wishing gate

Nikki Iles

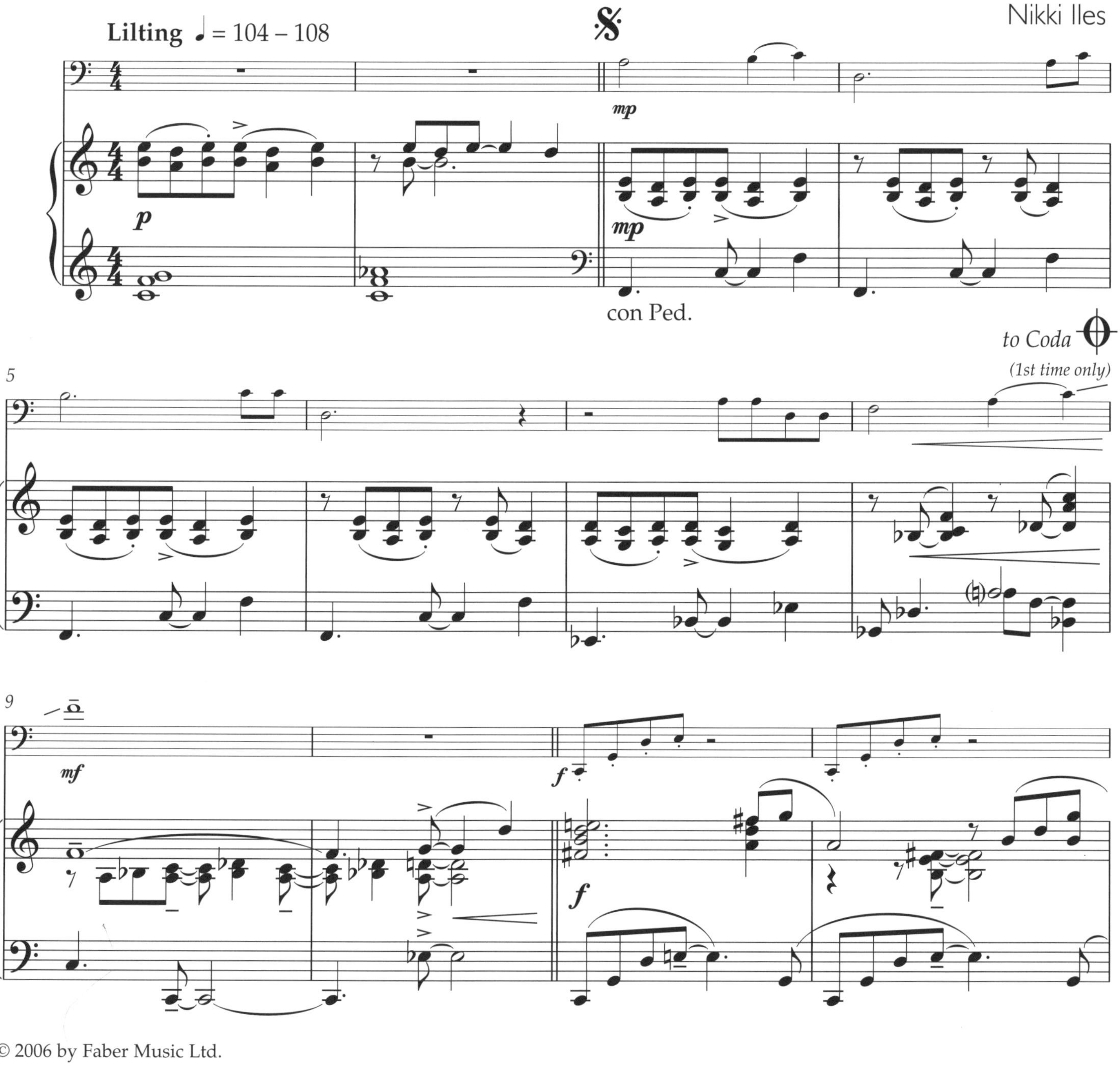

Lilting ♩ = 104 – 108

con Ped.

to Coda ⊕
(1st time only)

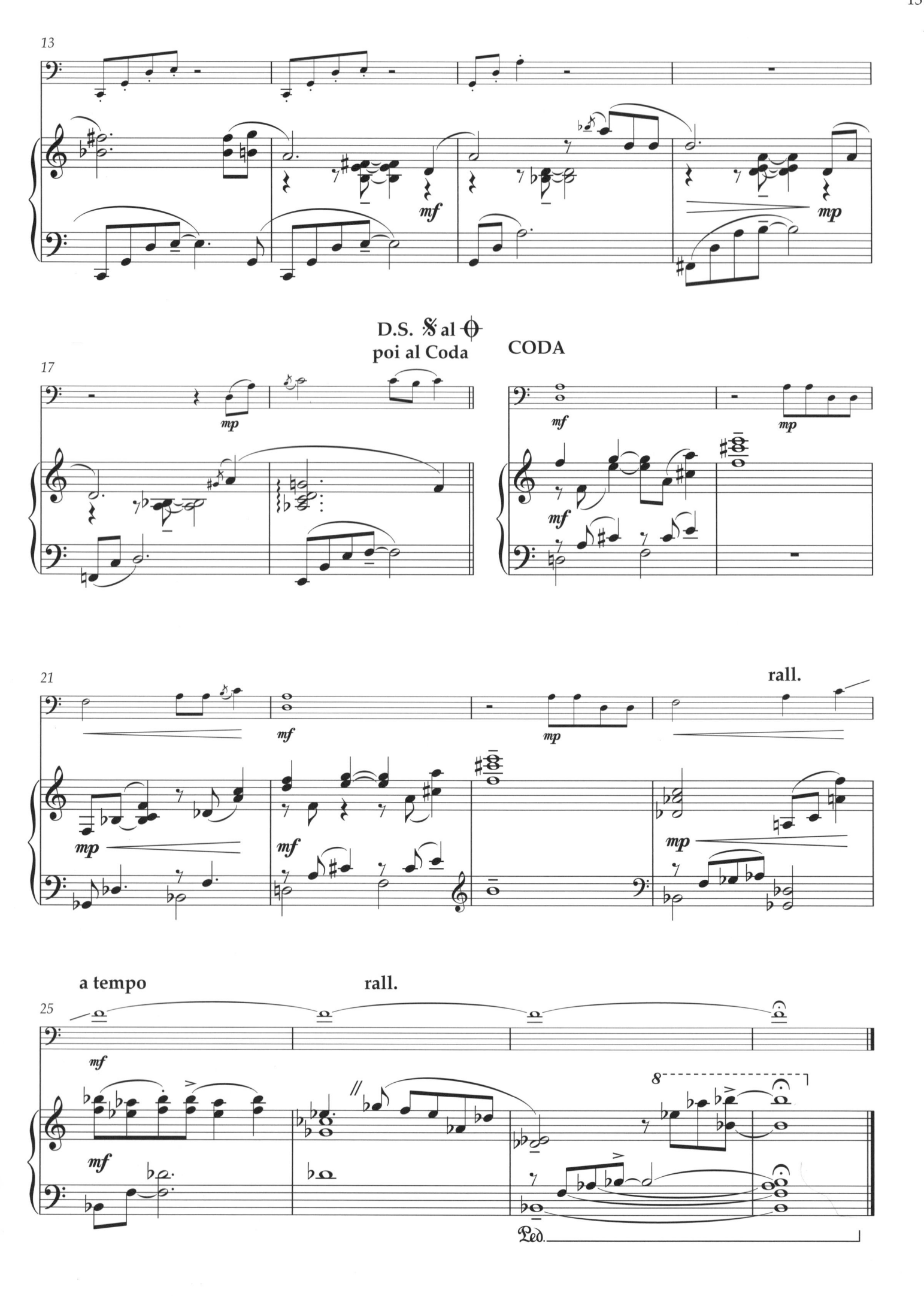

D.S. 𝄋 al ⊕
poi al Coda   CODA

Full name **Thomas Spencer Hewitt Jones**   *Date and place of birth* **24.10.84; Denmark Hill, London**
Favourite day of the week **Wednesday**   *Favourite drink* **raspberry smoothie**

Song of the rose

Thomas Hewitt Jones

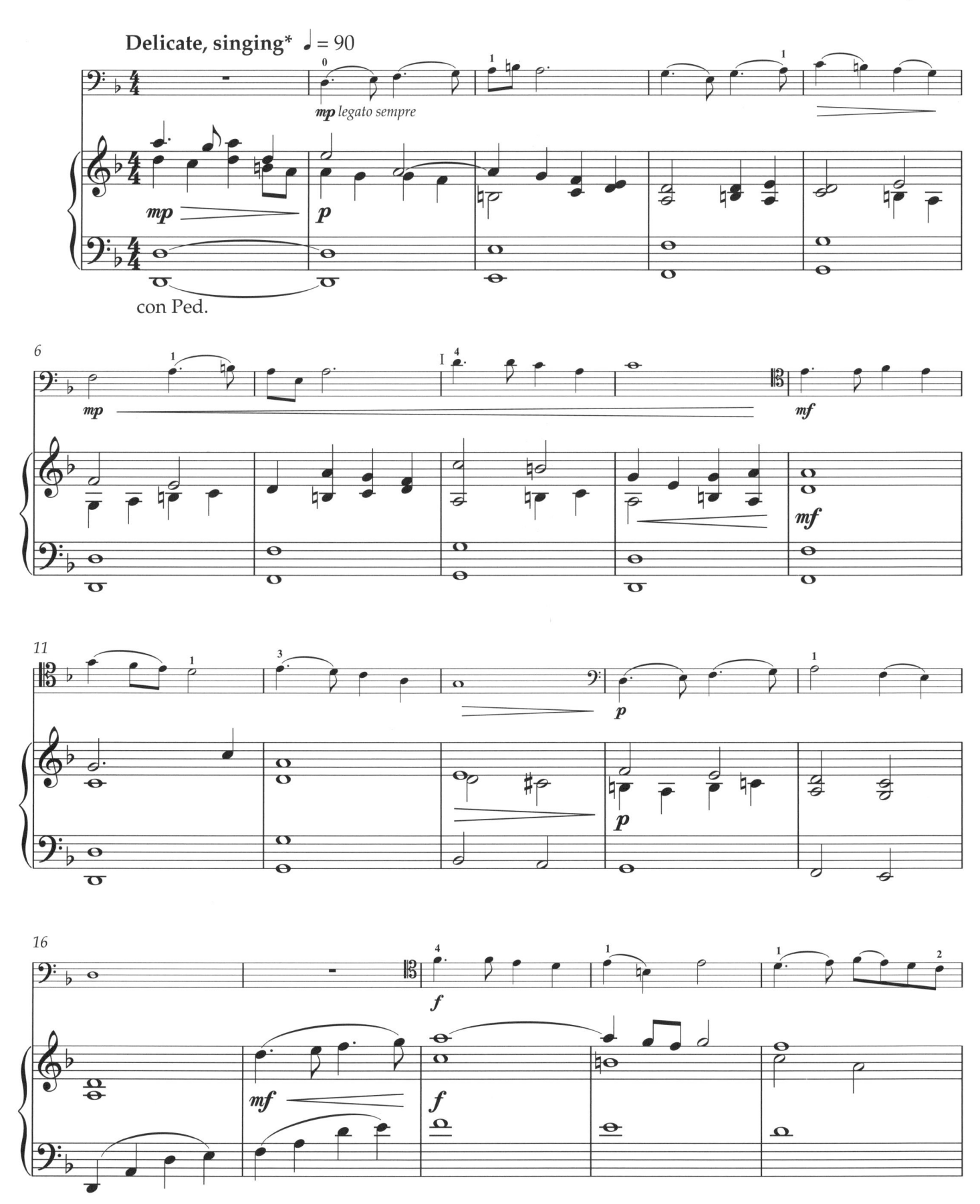

* Both the Cello and Piano should play molto legato throughout. Enjoy the long lines!

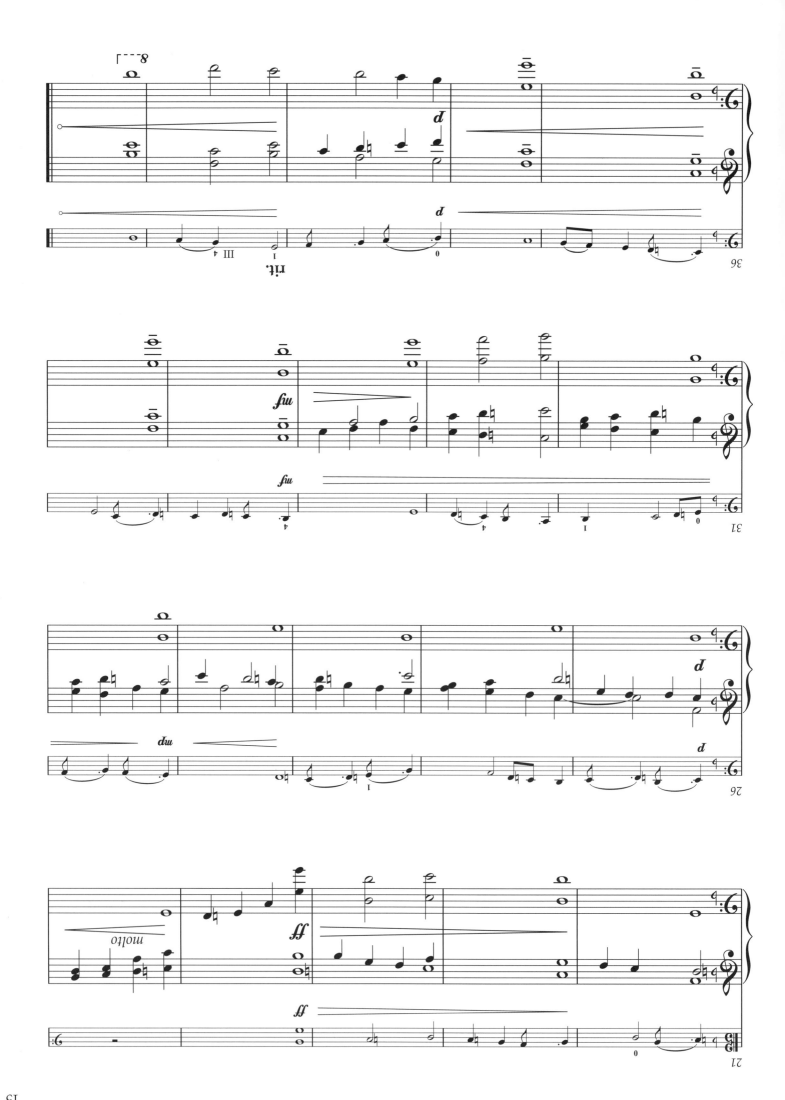

Full name **David John Matthews**   *Date and place of birth* **9.4.43; Walthamstow, London**
Favourite hobby **drawing**   *Favourite film* ***The Big Sleep***

Danny's dance

David Matthews

Sturdy and energetic ♩ = c.108

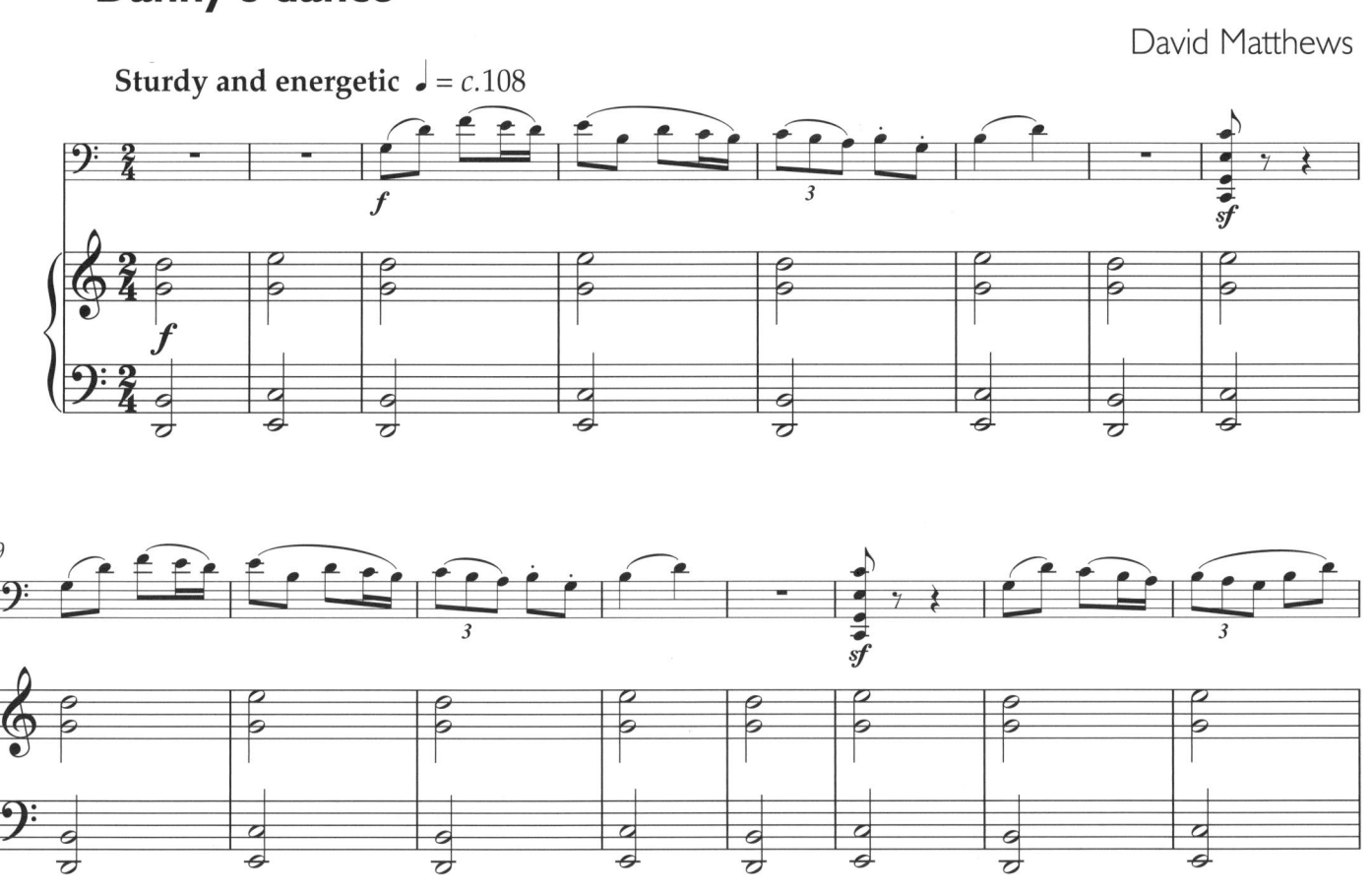

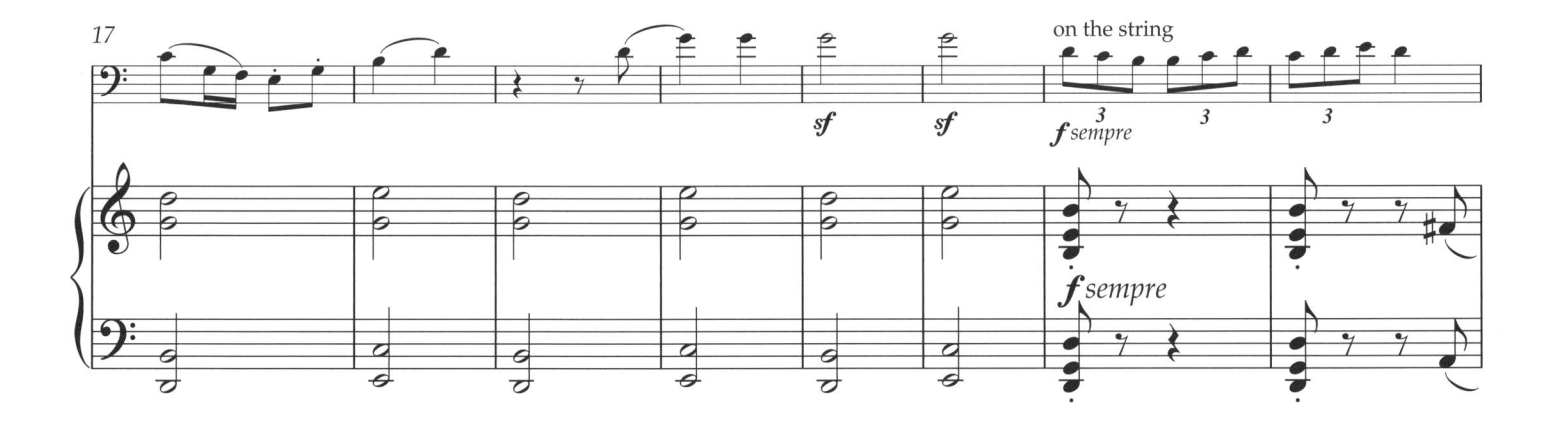

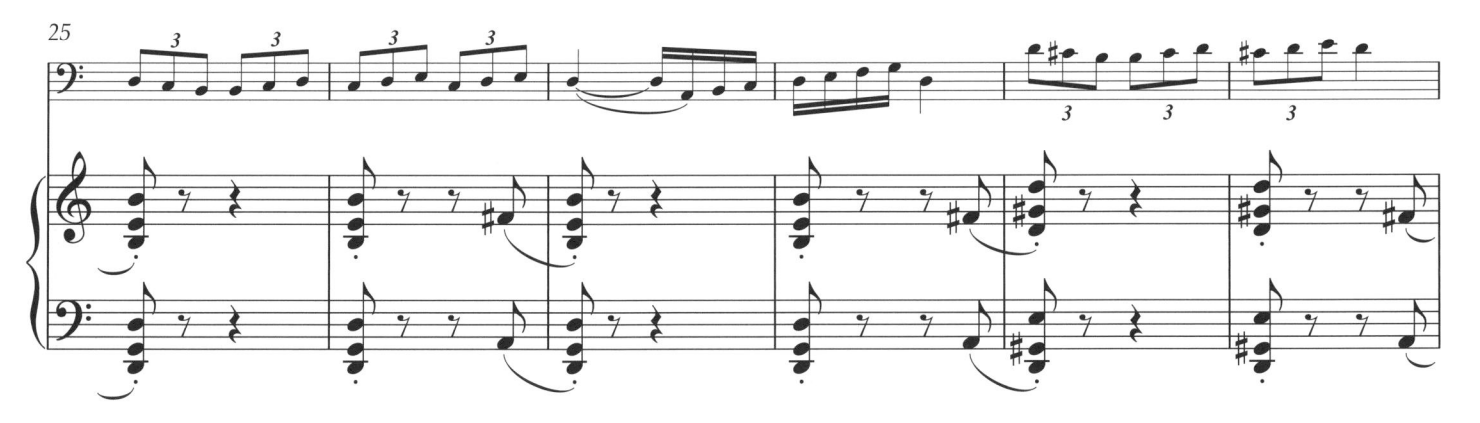

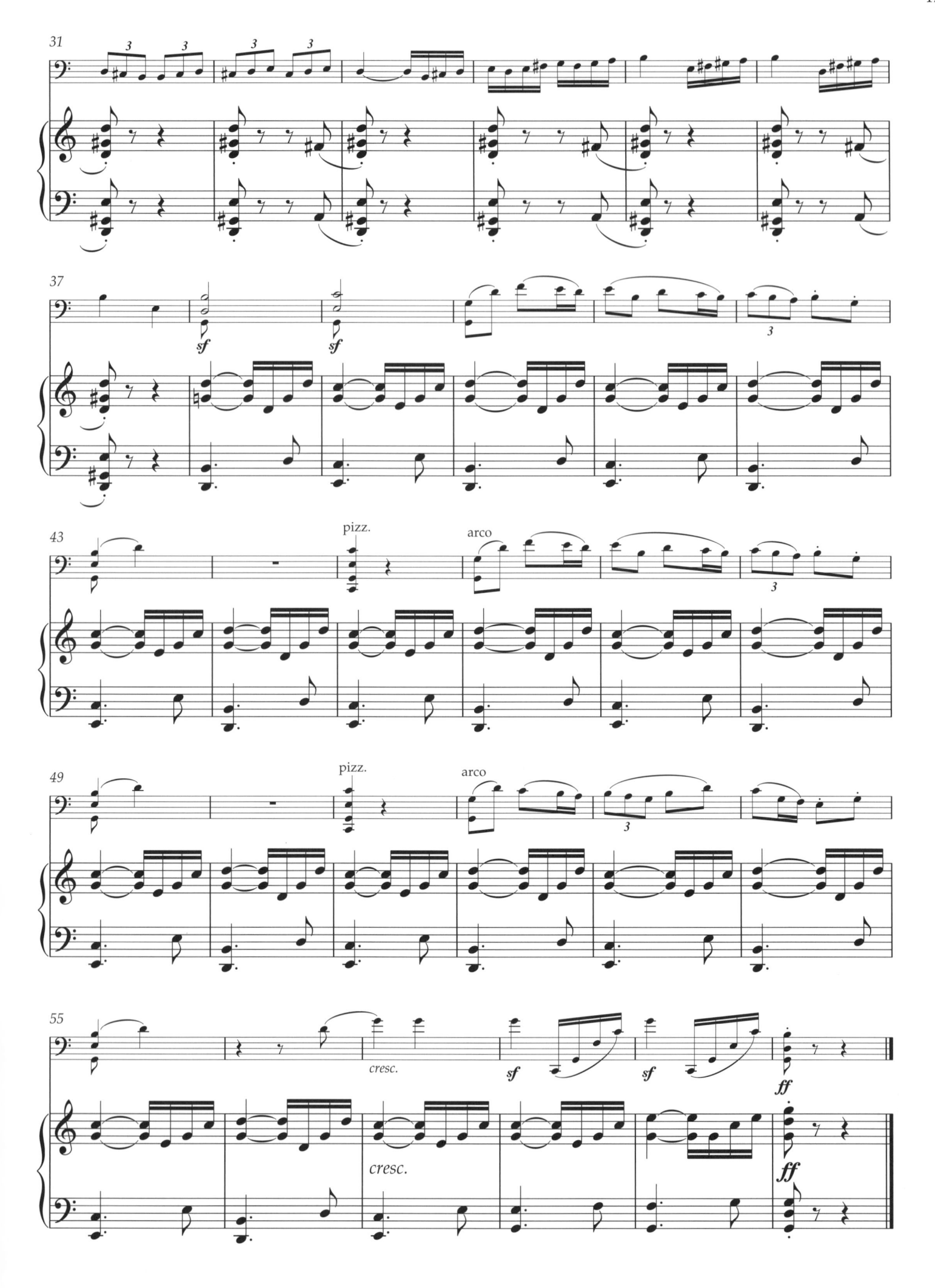

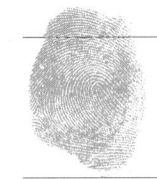

Full name **Elissa Milne**   *Date and place of birth* **2.8.67; Wahroonga, Sydney, Australia**
Favourite drink **Chinotto**
Favourite piece of music **'Toccata'** from Symphony No. 5 for Organ by Charles-Marie Widor

Ten toads

Elissa Milne

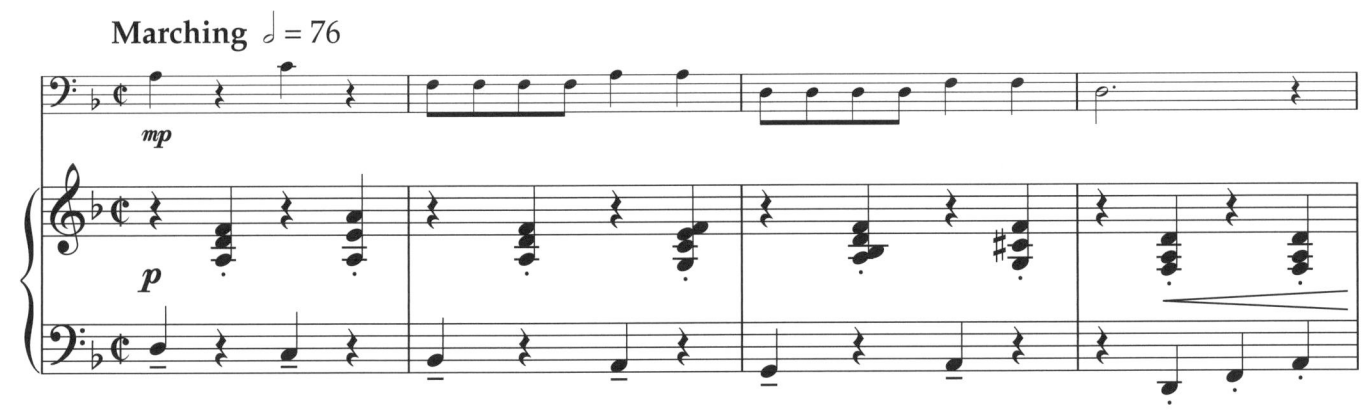

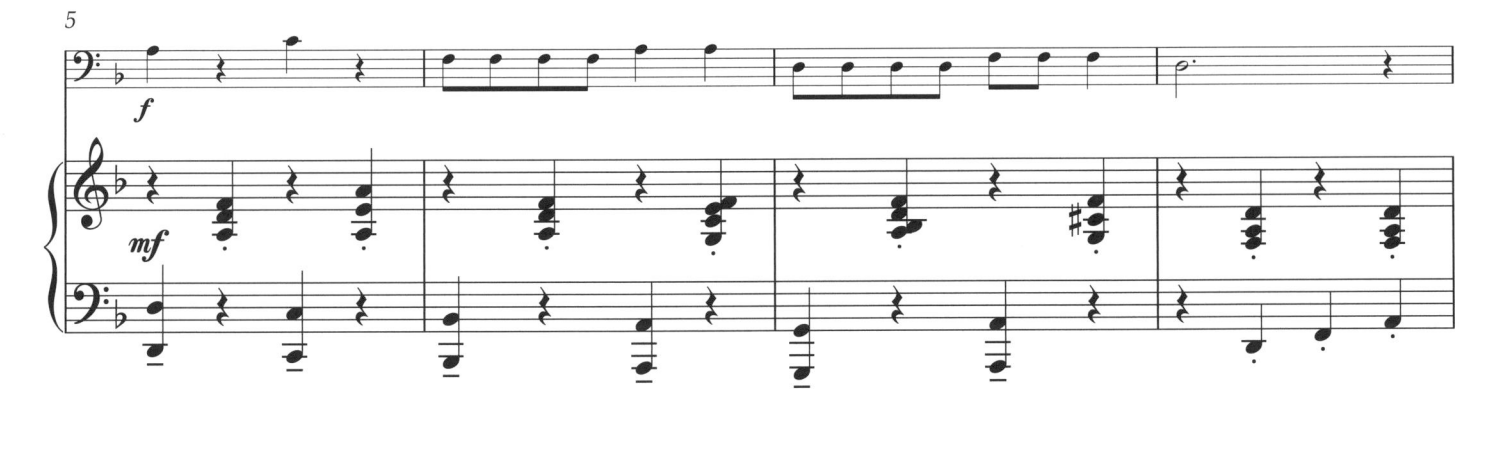

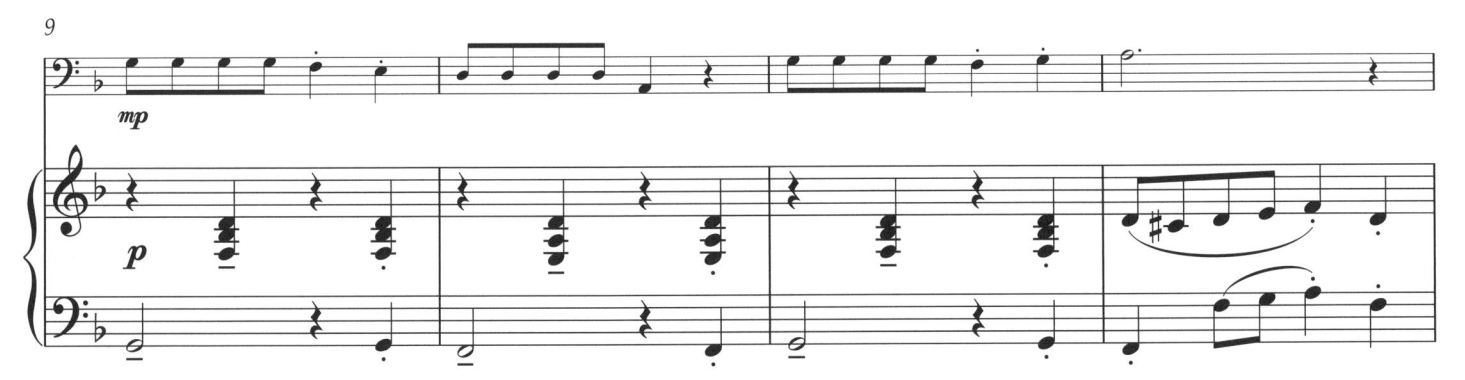

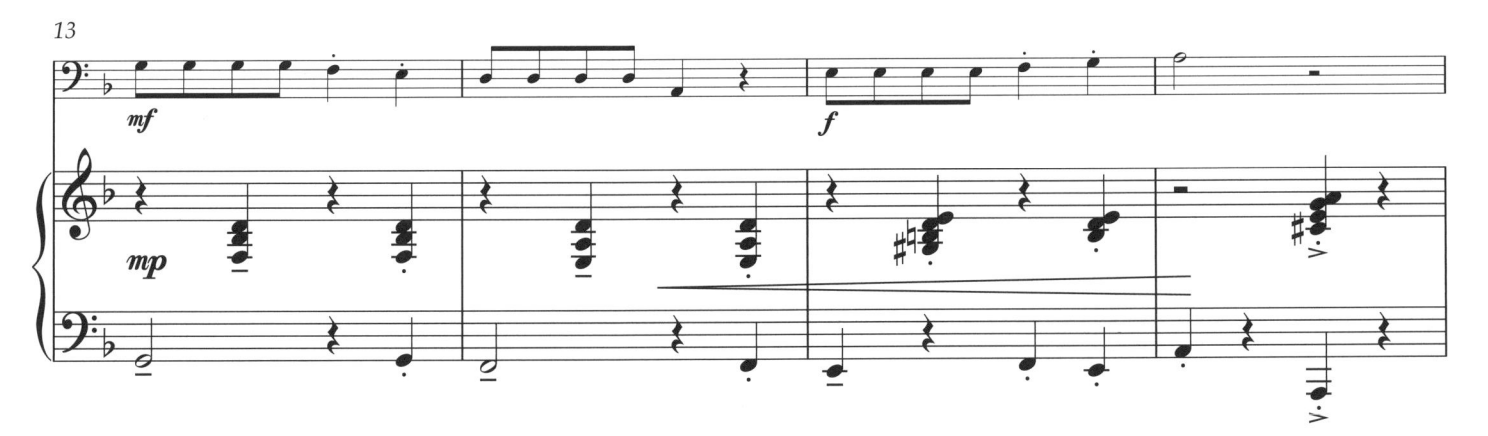

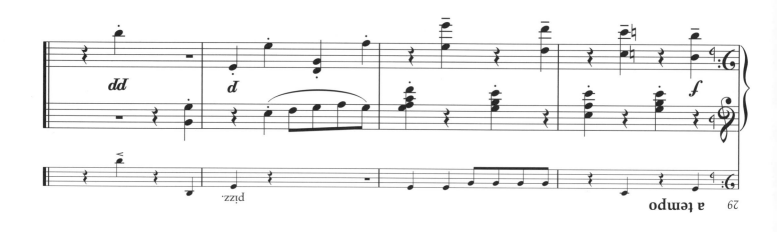
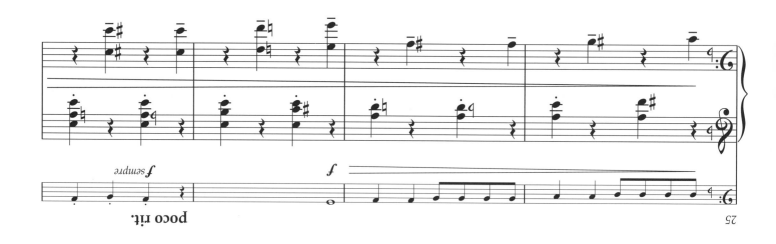
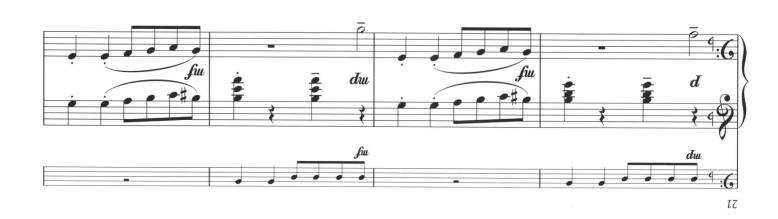
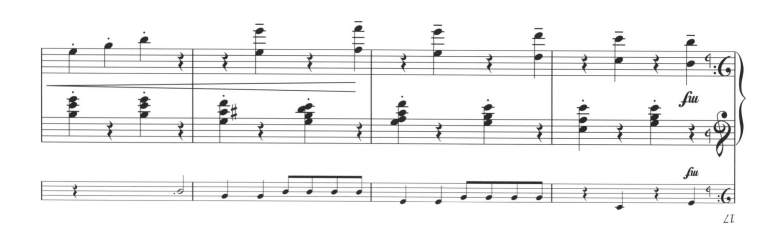

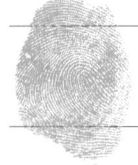

Full name **Christine Myers**   *Date and place of birth* **6.12.67**; Sydney, Australia
Favourite day of the week **Sunday**   *Favourite film* *The Visitors* (French comedy)

Shaky staircase

Christine Myers

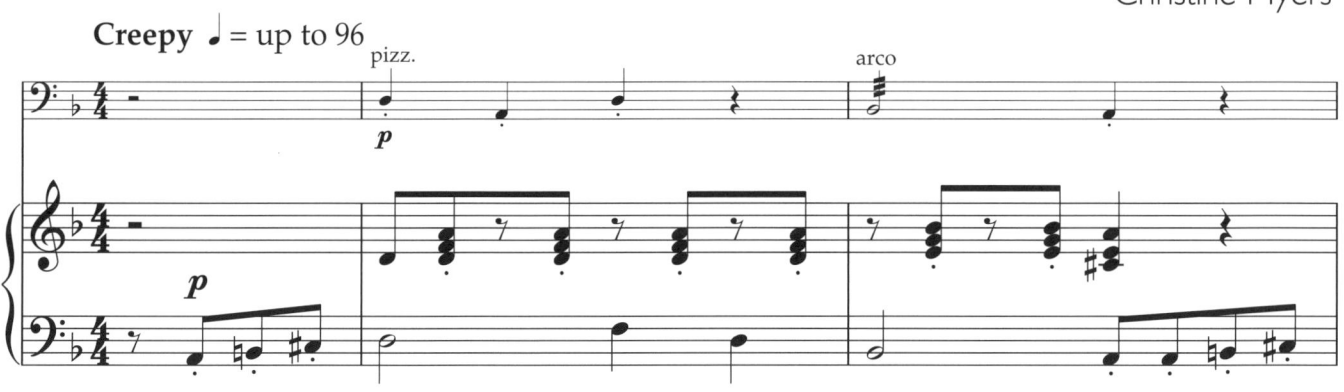

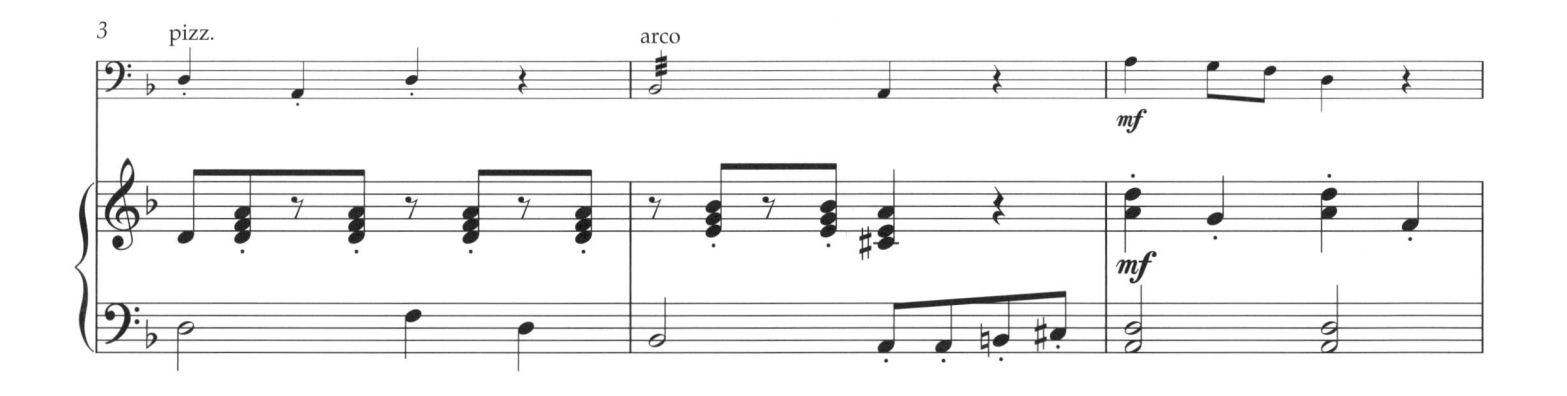

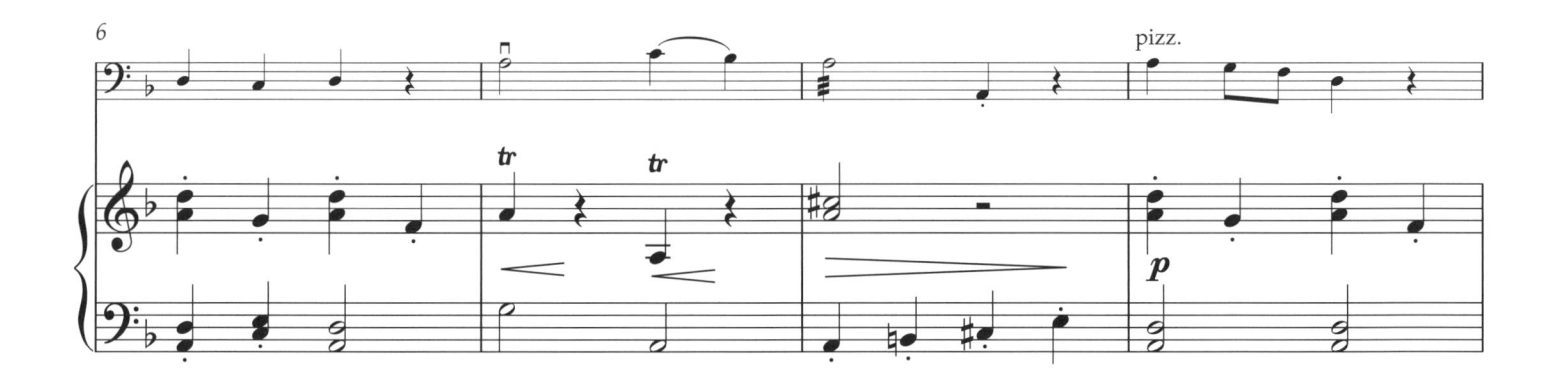

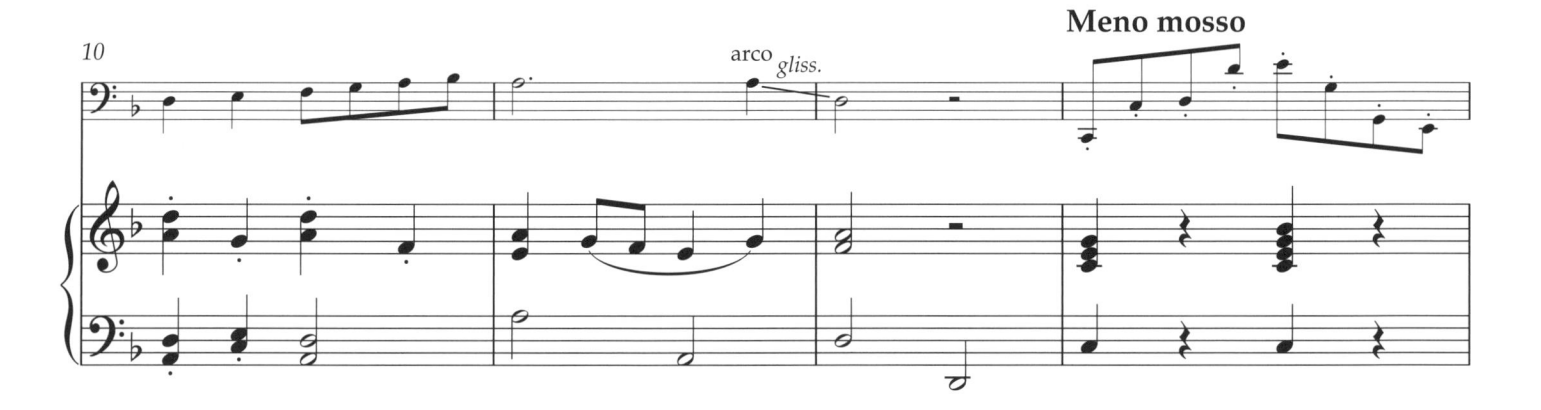

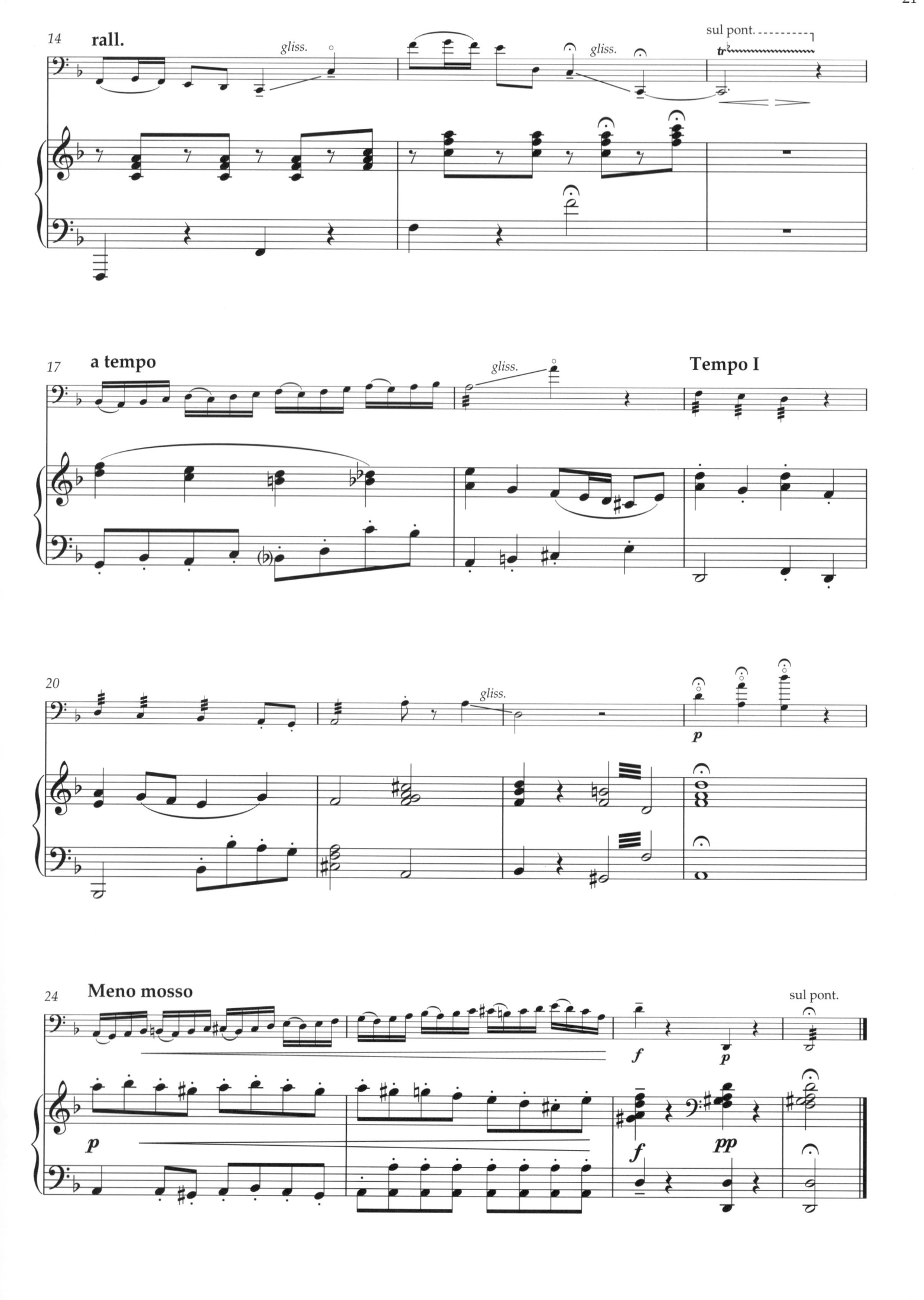

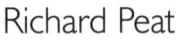

Full name **Richard Jeremy Peat**   *Date and place of birth* **25.5.79; Ramsgate**
Favourite pudding **apple crumble**   *Favourite colour* **blue**

Battle hymn

Richard Peat

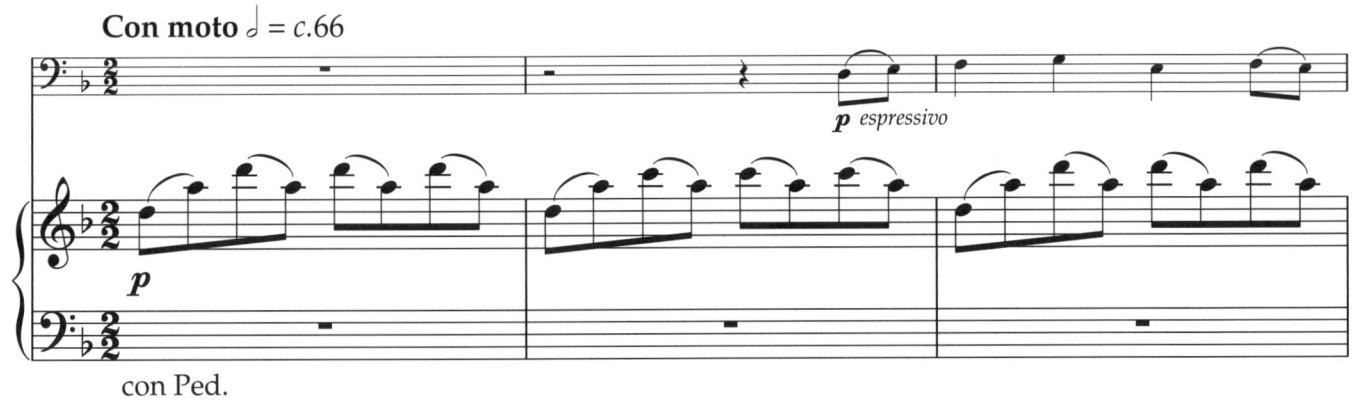

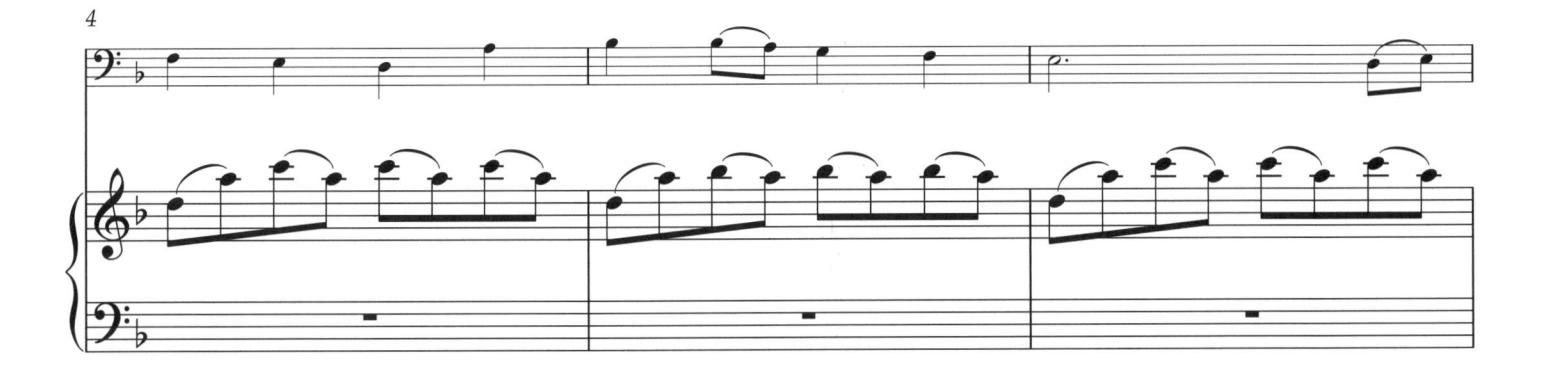

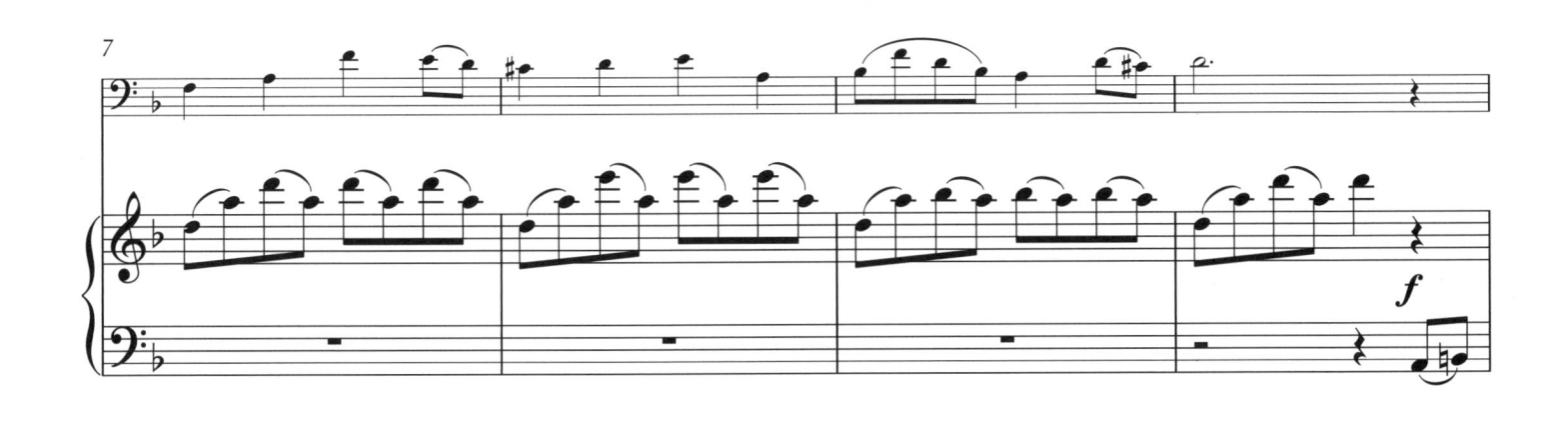

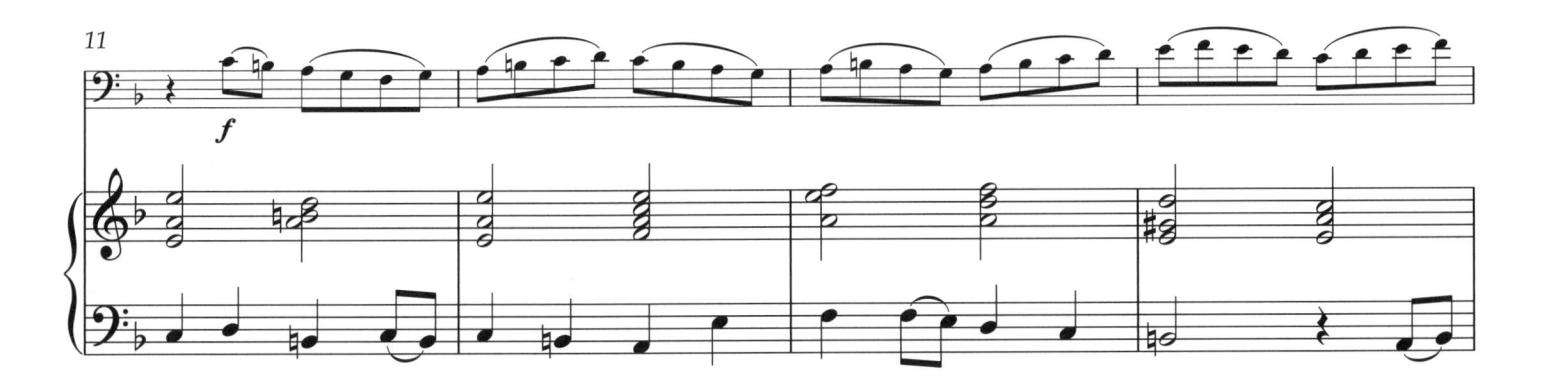

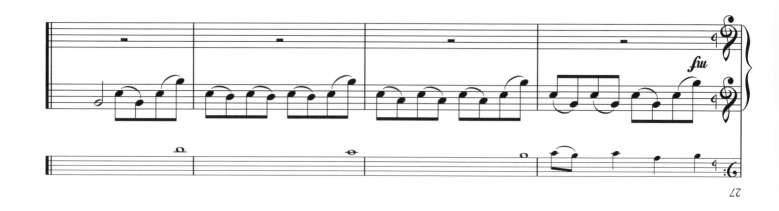

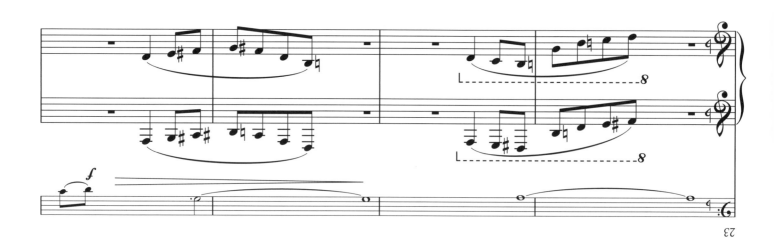

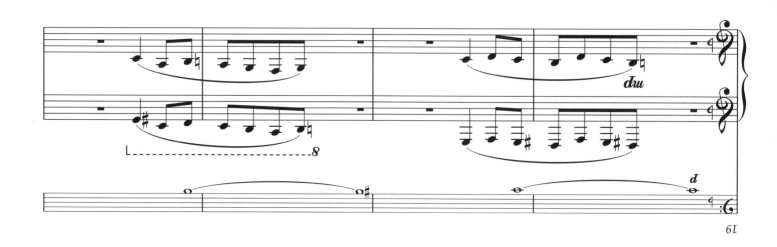

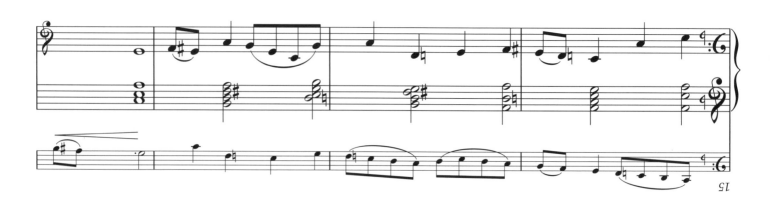

Full name **David John Matthews**　*Date and place of birth*　**9.4.43; Walthamstow, London**
Favourite hobby　**drawing**　*Favourite film*　*The Big Sleep*

Danny's dance

David Matthews

Sturdy and energetic ♩ = *c*.108

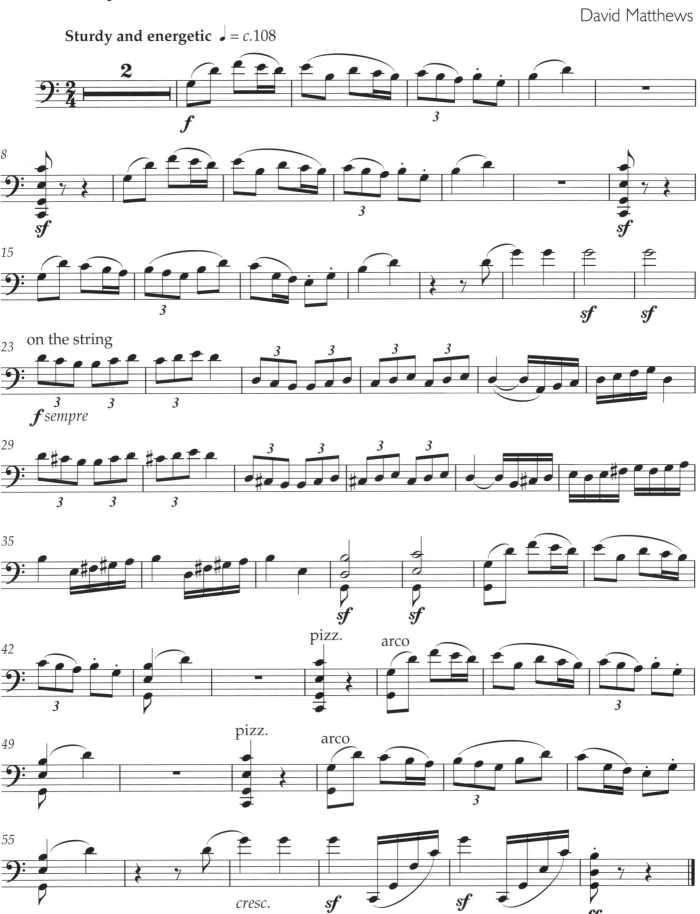

Full name **Elissa Milne**   *Date and place of birth* **2.8.67; Wahroonga, Sydney, Australia**
Favourite drink **Chinotto**
Favourite piece of music 'Toccata' from Symphony No. 5 for Organ by Charles-Marie Widor

Ten toads

Elissa Milne

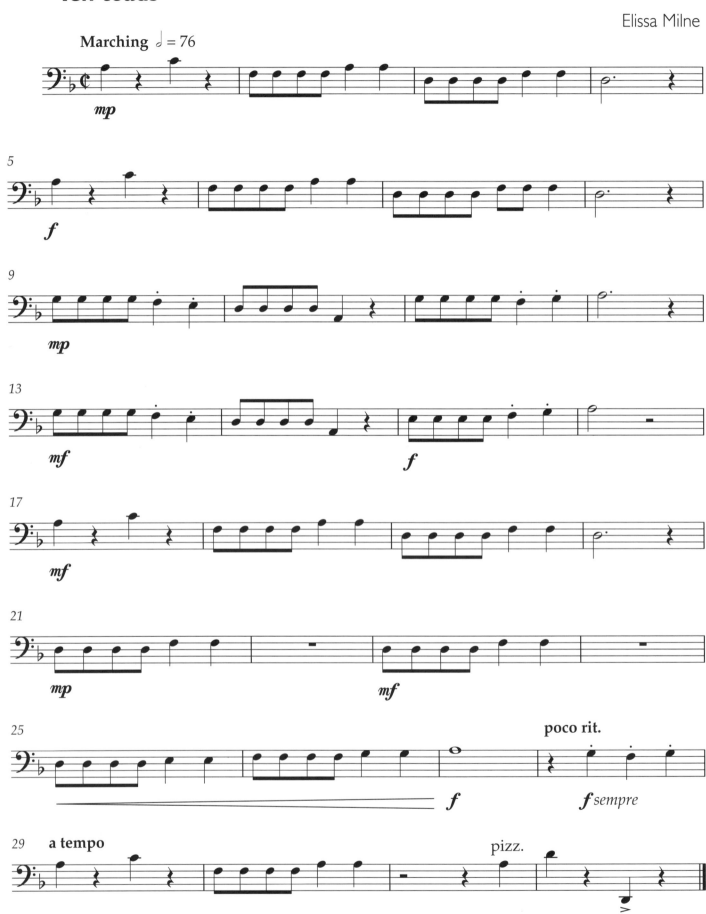

Full name **Christine Myers**   *Date and place of birth* **6.12.67; Sydney, Australia**
Favourite day of the week **Sunday**   *Favourite film* ***The Visitors*** **(French comedy)**

Shaky staircase

Christine Myers

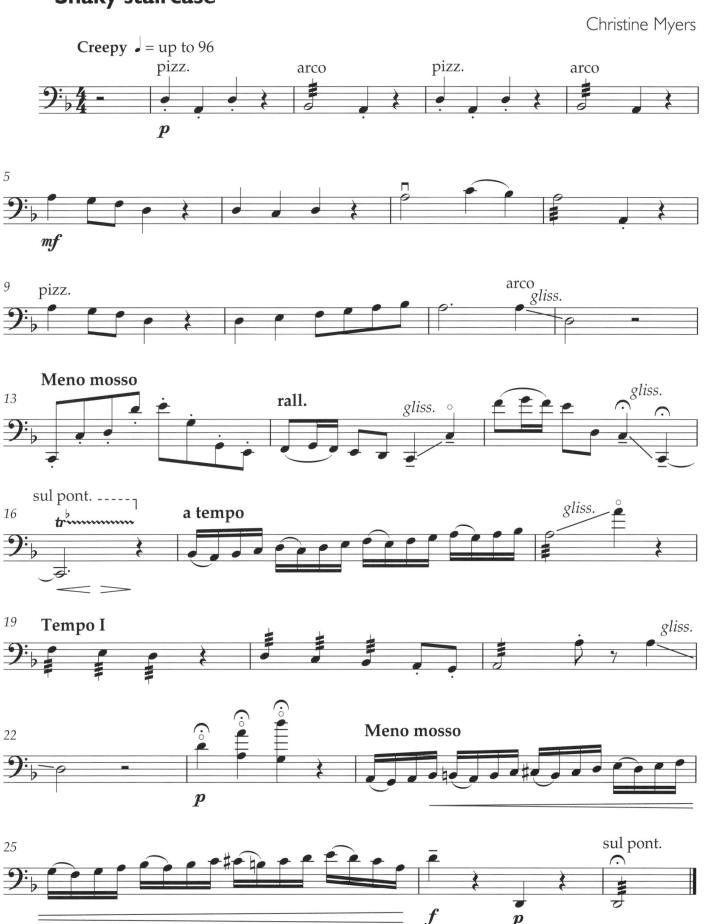

Full name **Richard Jeremy Peat** *Date and place of birth* **25.5.79; Ramsgate**
Favourite pudding **apple crumble** *Favourite colour* **blue**

Battle hymn

Richard Peat

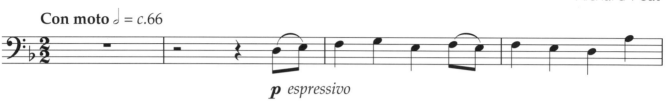

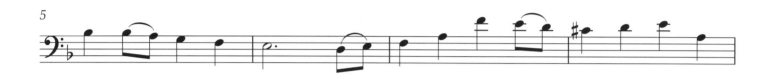

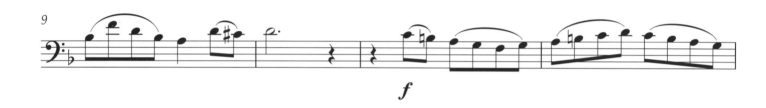

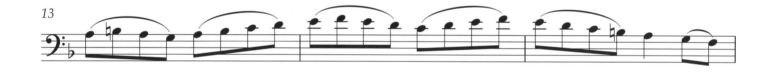

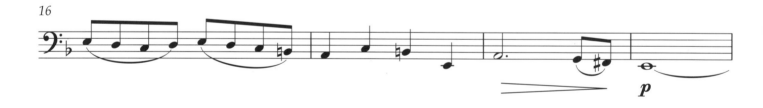

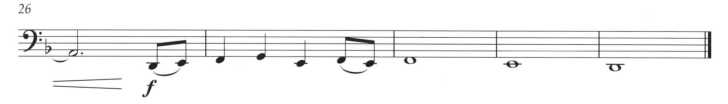